CONCENTRIC CIRCLES OF CONCERN

D0167258

CONCENTRIC CIRCLES OF CONCERN

Seven Stages for Making Disciples

W. Oscar Thompson
with Carolyn Thompson Ritzmann

Revised and Updated by Claude V. King

BROADMAN
&HOLMAN
PUBLISHERS

Nashville, Tennessee

0-8054-1959-4 (pbk.)

Published by: Broadman & Holman Publishers, Nashville, Tennessee
Editorial Team: Leonard G. Goss, John Landers, Sandra Bryer
Page Design and Typesetting: TF Designs, Mt. Juliet, Tennessee

Dewey Decimal Classification: 248
Subject Heading: EVANGELISM/CHRISTIAN LIFE

Scripture taken from the NEW AMERICAN STANDARD BIBLE.
© Copyright The Lockman Foundation, 1960, 1962, 1963, 1968, 1971,
1972, 1973, 1975, 1977, 1995.

Library of Congress Catologing-in-Publication Data

Thompson, W. Oscar, d. 1980.
    Concentric circles of concern: seven stages for making disciples
    / by W. Oscar Thompson, Jr. and Claude V. King.
        p. cm.
    Rev. and expanded by Claude V. King.
    ISBN 0-8054-1959-4 (pbk.)
    1. Witness bearing (Christianity) 2. Evangelistic work.
    I. King, Claude V., 1954–   . II. Title.
    BV4520.T57   1999
    248'5—dc21   99–30957
                                                          CIP

1 2 3 4 03 02 01 00 99

To my daughter, Damaris

I pray that the words of this book
will become reality in your life,
and may the words of The Book
continually be the word of our God
to your heart and life.

W. Oscar Thompson, Jr.

CONTENTS

Stage 5
Show Love: Show God's Love by Meeting Needs

Stage 6
Make Disciples: Make Disciples and Help Them Grow

Stage 7
Begin Again: Help New Christians Make Disciples

$\mathscr{I}$NTRODUCTION

by Claude V. King

Questions about Our Evangelistic Program

Prior to attending seminary in New Orleans, I served on the staff of a dynamic and evangelistic church in Nashville, Tennessee. I was trained in an evangelistic method that normally took teams to share the gospel with total strangers. We, however, were prepared to break the ice and establish some sort of relationship prior to talking about the person's spiritual needs. I am very grateful for that training experience because I studied the Scriptures and came to better understand what faith in Christ means. I learned how to use God's Word to tell others about his conditions for their salvation.

After going through the training course several times, I wound up leading the course for a while. From that perspective I made some new discoveries. Though we did see a number of people pray to receive Christ in their homes, very few ever followed through with a public commitment to Christ. We were not very effective at helping these people get established in a local body of Christ where they could grow.

We did see many adults make public professions of their faith in Christ. However, most of these did not come directly from our evangelistic visitation program. I noticed that most of these people were family, relatives, neighbors, or friends of our members. People who had learned to share the gospel with others were being used by God to lead people in their circles of influence to Christ. These were the people we were able to effectively assimilate into the church.

We didn't really plan for this type of outreach. It happened only as God's people were led to share the gospel with the people they were closest to. Our planned evangelism strategy served primarily to prepare and equip people for sharing Christ. God took them from that point and used them in sharing through their relationships. When I realized the reality of what was happening, I felt uneasy about the fact that our greatest evangelist fruit came not from our evangelistic program but through unplanned experiences of our members.

CONCENTRIC CIRCLES OF CONCERN

While I was attending seminary in the early 1980s, I came across *Concentric Circles of Concern* at the bookstore. As I began to read the experiences of Oscar and Carolyn Thompson, I kept thinking, "This is it!" *Concentric Circles* explained what God was doing through relationships in my previous church. I began to wonder why this book was not required reading for every seminary student. For me, it explained in moving ways how I could guide God's people to share Christ in a very natural way with the people they knew and loved. I saw how I could help people be used by God to show his love and see loved ones drawn to Jesus.

When I began to develop and write curriculum resources for lay discipleship, I came across two types of books. One could be very inspiring and informational but did not motivate me to change. It was like preaching an evangelistic message and then never giving an invitation for response.

The other type motivated me to apply what I was learning. Then in a small group context, other Christians could help me follow through in the application in ways that thoroughly changed my life. As I watched what God did through courses like *Experiencing God, Fresh Encounter,* and *The Mind of Christ,* I developed a conviction that book writers should regularly give an invitation for a reader to respond and apply the truths being taught.

For many years I've wanted to revise *Concentric Circles of Concern* to do just that. The message has so impacted my own life that I sensed God would use it in even greater ways as Christians helped each other apply the message to their own lives and ministries. This is what we pray will happen as you study this revised edition of *Concentric Circles of Concern*.

SEVEN STAGES FOR MAKING DISCIPLES

After studying Oscar's original message, I identified seven stages that he guided students to work through in reaching their world with the gospel. To help you see those stages more clearly, I've added those seven stages to the original Concentric Circles diagram. Now I invite you to walk through those stages in your own relationships. Oscar will teach you, with the help of the Holy Spirit, to develop the kind of lifestyle through which God can show his love to those around you.

Personalizing the Chapters

At the end of each chapter, I've added some questions and activities to help you make personal application of the truths in your life and relationships. These activities will guide you to do what Oscar has taught.

One of my favorite Scriptures related to this process is Proverbs 16:3. "Commit thy works unto the Lord, and thy thoughts shall be established" (KJV). In other words, do the right things and you will experience God working through you in such a way that you will change your mind and attitudes as well. We usually take the opposite approach. We try to change our thinking before reforming our actions. God can work both ways, but sometimes obedience and doing are the best ways to get your thinking in line with God's ways. As you begin personalizing these truths by completing the activities, you will experience God working through your relationships to touch others for Christ. When you experience God in that way, your thinking and attitudes and actions will move in line with what God is doing.

Small-Group Study Helps

Another addition to this revised work is the small-group activities section at the end of each chapter. I've titled these activities "Building Up the Body."

God created us for relationships. When we come to Christ, he places us in the body of Christ because we need each other. We can and should "stimulate one another to love and good deeds" (Heb. 10:24). I highly recommend that you not read and study this book alone. Get a small group of other Christians to go through the study with you. By sharing and praying together, you will find that God will teach you things you would never learn alone. You will experience God working through your group to see others come to Christ.

You can study *Concentric Circles of Concern* at your own pace. If you use it as a supplement for an ongoing group like a Sunday School class, you may want to read and process one chapter each week. During your weekly class time, you can spend a few minutes sharing experiences and praying for each other. If you use the book as a specific training tool for lifestyle evangelism, you may want to study three or four chapters at a time. In this case, you would combine the small-group learning activities for each of the chapters covered by your group session.

THE FRINGE BENEFIT OF KOINONIA

I believe you will also experience one fringe benefit from studying this book with others. As you share and pray with each other about your relationships, you will develop a close fellowship with your fellow Christians. This is the *koinonia* (close love and fellowship) that God has intended for his people all along. Somehow, we have lost that experience in the busy lifestyles of modern life. God wants to restore that experience of love and fellowship to his people in our day. I pray you will experience the fullest dimensions of the love of Christ, together "with all the saints" (Eph. 3:18–19).

AN ILLUSTRATION FROM ARKANSAS

Earlier this year, while I was in Arkansas for a meeting, the host pastor testified to his church's experience of the reality of how God works through relationships to show love and draw people to faith in Christ. At that time, I sensed that God wanted ALL his people to be equipped to experience his power and presence in similar ways. This revised volume comes with my prayer that you, your small group, and your church will experience God's saving grace flowing through relationships in ever increasing dimensions.

The pastor in Arkansas gave me the following report. A young couple had come to Christ some months prior to this time. One Sunday the pastor asked, "How are you doing?"

"Our car got stolen this week," they responded. "We need your help. The police want us to file charges in case they find the person who stole the car. But we're new Christians, and we don't know what the Bible has to say about that. What should we do?"

The pastor explained the role of government in maintaining order and punishing wrongdoers. He suggested that they go ahead and file charges and begin praying for the person who stole their car. "This person probably is not a Christian, and God may want to do something through this experience to bring him to Christ," the pastor suggested.

They began praying. A month later they received a call that their car had been found, and a fifteen-year-old boy was in jail. They visited him in jail. They were so excited to meet him, and they told him how they had been praying for him for a whole month. That probably was not the response he expected.

In talking with the young man, they found out his mother was in the hospital. They visited her to show God's love. She told them that she had lost her home because of financial problems, and she had nowhere to go when she was released from the hospital. This young couple took her home with them and began to meet her needs.

When the members of the church found out, they decided to help. They knew the young couple was not financially able to do what they were doing, so they pitched in and helped get the mother into a furnished apartment. She was overwhelmed by the love of this couple whose car had been stolen by her son. She placed her faith in Jesus Christ and was converted. Then she began sharing Christ with her son, and he was converted.

While all this was happening, her ex-husband was released from prison. He came home looking for his family. You see, he had become a Christian while he was in prison and had been taking Bible correspondence courses, sensing God's calling into some kind of ministry. He came home to see if there was any possibility that he could be reconciled with his family. Doesn't that sound just like something God would do? In fact, only he could orchestrate circumstances in such a way that all these things happened at just the right time.

Thank God for a young couple who fell in love with the Lord and decided to make him Lord of their lives. Now a little church in Arkansas is overwhelmed at what they have experienced of God's power to transform lives through demonstrated love.

My prayer in revising *Concentric Circles of Concern* is that we all will become active participants in a mighty harvest as God works through us to make disciples of the nations of the earth.

BIOGRAPHICAL NOTE

Oscar Thompson taught personal evangelism to seminary students prior to dying of cancer in 1980. Although Oscar had begun work on *Concentric Circles of Concern,* his wife Carolyn compiled the manuscript of the first edition (1980) following his death. I wish to thank Carolyn and her daughter Damaris for permitting me to participate in this revision.

Chapter One

$\mathscr{T}$HE $\mathscr{I}$MPORTANCE OF $\mathscr{R}$ELATIONSHIPS

Jim came into my office one day and said, "Dr. Thompson, my dad is a nominal Christian; but when he learned that I was going into the ministry, he became furious. He told me that he did not mind my being a Christian, but he did not want me to become a 'religious nut.'"

Jim's father drove a truck for a big truck line, owned his own rig, and wanted his son to follow in his footsteps. It was somewhat of a family tradition. Instead, Jim came to the seminary. As a result, Jim's relationship with his parents was ruptured.

"We had been very close until this happened," Jim explained. "Since then I have just ignored them, as they have ignored me. It has been a hurt to me, but I am going to serve Jesus. My family can do whatever they please."

I asked, "Jim, do you really think you can be right with God and have ruptured relationships with your parents? You need to meet their needs. You need to love them."

Jim answered, "Well, that's right, but I don't know what to do."

So I suggested, "Get the bitterness straight in your own heart and then start to pray for them, Jim. Right those ruptured relationships."

Jim began to pray for his dad and mom. That same day he came to class brokenhearted and said, "Friends, just please pray for me." Then Jim prayed, "Father, I do not even know if my daddy knows you. But, Father, I have been wrong in my attitude toward my parents. Forgive me of my attitude, and help me meet my parents' needs."

Jim wrote a letter to his parents, asking them to forgive him for his bitterness and the broken relationship. He told them that he loved them.

The next day, before the letter had time to reach his parents, Jim received a telephone call from his dad. Jim's dad had never before had a

7

route to Dallas, but he said, "Son, I have a route to Dallas this week, and I want to see you."

"Oh, Dad, that's great!"

On that Saturday afternoon, a big rig pulled up in front of Jim's dorm. When Jim opened the dorm door, his tall father stood with tears trickling down his cheeks. "Jim, I am wrong with God," he said. "Can you help me?"

THE MOST IMPORTANT WORD

I believe the most important word in the English language, apart from proper nouns, is *relationship*. You say, "But *love* has to be the most important word."

I ask you, though, where is love going to be if there is no relationship? Relationship is the track. Love is what rolls over the track. Love moves through a relationship. But the thing that satisfies the deepest longing of your being is a relationship with someone.

You may think you want to be a Henry David Thoreau and go to a secluded Walden Pond to get away from the world. But Thoreau did not stay there forever and neither could you. Why? There is something in the nature of people—something built into people—that desires to be wanted, to be needed, to be fulfilled. Those desires are fulfilled only in relationships.

In the relationships of life, we must have an inner relationship. We cannot go off somewhere by ourselves. However, if we cannot get along with people, going off by ourselves may seem best. But we will not be fulfilled because something in our nature cries out for fellowship.

Rare is the individual who wants to be a loner. In being a loner, a person loses the purpose for existence because God wants to reveal his character through a Christian's life. He does this by loving through you in your relationships with others.

John said, "What we have seen and heard we proclaim to you also, that you also may have fellowship with us; and indeed our fellowship is with the Father, and with His Son Jesus Christ" (1 John 1:3).

RIGHT RELATIONSHIPS

Consider all of the warm wonderful times of joy and happiness. Do you remember:

• The warm caress of your parents' hands;

- The giggles and laughter as you romped with your friends or brothers and sisters in the bright sunshine of a summer afternoon;
- The joy of your first date with that bright-eyed boy or girl;
- The look of enthusiasm in those with whom you work?

All these relationships make you what you are. Right relationships with parents leave you mentally and emotionally ready for marriage or for a baby brought into the family—new relationships. The special days of happiness—birthday, anniversary, Thanksgiving, Christmas—are fulfilling because of warm, wonderful relationships. Right relationships allow you to experience the best life has to offer.

Home Is the School for Relationships

God established the home before any other institution. The home is the basic institution in which God seeks to teach the sacredness of relationships and how to establish and nourish them. The home is the only institution designed to teach relationships. When this institution fails, a child is left mentally, emotionally, and spiritually crippled.

The home under God should be the place to learn about relationships—husband and wife, parent and child, brother and sister. Here is where a person learns to love—learns to meet needs. A helpless baby placed in the hands of parents helps the parents to mature and develop their ability to love, to meet needs. A child is taught to submit his wayward, self-centered will to the will of the parents. Here selfishness, which is the root of sin, matures into a discipline to build relationships and meet the needs of others.

God has designed the home to be the school of relationships. The dearest, the closest, the most intimate human relationship that must exist is between husband and wife. Through the relationship of husband and wife, we teach our children about relationships. This is our own school of relationships.

Broken Relationships

A little more reflection about the importance of relationships will lead to some more obvious but amazing conclusions. Think about the crisis times of your life:

- As a child separated from your parents;
- As a child angry with your parents;
- As a teenager breaking up with your sweetheart;
- The resentment and misunderstanding that separated you from a friend;

- Perhaps the loss of a parent or spouse—remember the emptiness, the heartbreak;
- An argument with your husband or wife—maybe even divorce;
- A crisis with an employee or employer;
- Times of resentment and rupture with family;
- The distress in business or in your church.

List all the dark, sad, unhappy times in your life, and you will see that the vast majority of these times was created by ruptured, strained, or broken relationships.

Every broken business, every broken home, every broken friendship is a broken relationship. Expand this to city, national, or international problems, to every crime committed, to every war from the beginning of time that has brought untold broken hopes, lives, and dreams resulting from wrong relationships.

When society ceases to treasure relationships, it becomes decadent. Manners become course and cheap. Common courtesy is soon forgotten. Hearts become thankless, ceasing to show appreciation. As human history so painfully demonstrates, bad relationships produce:

- broken marriages;
- broken homes;
- unsuccessful businesses;
- divided churches;
- weak governments;
- chaotic nations.

RESTORED RELATIONSHIPS

Solve the relationship problems and there would be no divorce, no war, no employer-employee or labor-management disputes. Solve the relationship problems of the world, and humanity's most perplexing problems would be solved since right relationships produce:

- solid marriages;
- stable homes;
- successful businesses;
- ministering churches;
- good governments;
- strong nations.

THE BODY OF CHRIST IS A DIVINE HOSPITAL

We know that God wants to meet our needs. He builds beautiful relationships in the body of Christ. He intends that we love one another the way he loved us. He wants to meet our needs through the body of Christ so that we will all be healthy parts of a functioning body. We need each other.

Jesus came to earth to meet our deepest need. He died on the cross to redeem the earth to himself. He ascended to heaven, and he left his earthly body on earth to go out to enlarge and strengthen the body of believers.

Let's say the church is the divine hospital. The world is so very full of sickness. Many people come to the hospital for help, and every church that is doing what it needs to be doing realizes that we all continually need help. We come, over and again, for help, and we receive it. The only tragedy is that if we do not mature and join the hospital staff and start meeting other people's needs, we become a liability, and the flow is always going inward. So we stagnate, and that hurts us. That hurts the body of Christ.

After we have come for help and have received it, God wants us to go out and build relationships with others. Then we will become part of the helping staff. As we reach out to meet another's needs, we find our own needs are met.

MY PURPOSE FOR THIS BOOK

Dear friend, if your life is in turmoil today, I venture to say it is because of a ruptured relationship with someone. One purpose of this book is to explore the possible causes of your broken relationships and show how they can be mended. In other words, it is written to help meet your needs.

I want to help you experience restored relationships and begin to experience the best life has to offer. Not only will right relationships be a blessing to you, but they will also be a blessing to others around you. Your family will be blessed. Your friends, relatives, and coworkers will be blessed.

The key to a fulfilled life is relationships. Things do not satisfy; relationships do. The first relationship is with the Father. When he becomes Lord of our lives, we forfeit forever the right to choose whom we will love, and he releases his love in us to build right relationships.

Recall the story about Jim and his dad at the beginning of the chapter. When Jim got right with God, he also wanted to get right with his parents. Once God had Jim prepared, he brought Jim's dad to Dallas so that

Jim's life could be a channel of love to point his dad to Jesus Christ. That's the way God works.

All this is why I contend that the most important word in the English language is *relationship*. Through right relationships, God's love can flow to be a blessing to all the lives it touches. Will you allow God to use your life and your relationships as a channel for his love to flow to others?

"Yes," you say? Wonderful! In the next chapter we'll take a look at God's plan to bless a world through his people.

PERSONALIZING CHAPTER 1

Using a journal or notebook, respond to the following questions or activities. Record details that will help you understand and apply the truths of this chapter to your own life.

1. Pray and ask the Lord to teach you about the importance of relationships. If you have a relationship that needs to be reconciled, like Jim and his dad, ask God to guide you to be reconciled. Ask him for the courage to make things right.
2. List two or three of the most happy or joyful experiences of your life, and identify one person who was involved in those experiences with you.
3. List two of the most dark, sad, or unhappy experiences of your life, and write the initials of a person who was involved in those experiences with you.
4. List the "top five" memorable or significant relationships with people you have ever had in your life.
5. If you could improve or be reconciled in one relationship in your life today, which one would it be? With whom? What do you sense God would have you do to get that relationship right? Ask him.

BUILDING UP THE BODY

Use the following questions and activities with your small group to help one another apply these truths to your lives and to build up the body of Christ.

1. Invite volunteers to share one or more of the following:
   - One of my most joyful and happy experiences growing up was . . .
   - One of the darkest, saddest, unhappy times in my past was . . .
   - One of my most significant positive relationships with another person is (or was) . . .

2. Discuss ways your home life growing up has affected your successes or failures in relationships. What are some of the positive lessons you learned about relationships?

3. Discuss ways your church experience has (or could have) provided a "divine hospital" for the healing of relationships. How do you sense a small-group study of this book may help?

4. Invite volunteers to tell about any relationship God has identified that needs to be reconciled. Take time to pray with each person who shares that God will guide him or her to experience reconciliation.

5. Take time to pray for each other in one or more of the following areas:
   - thanksgiving for meaningful relationships of the past
   - spiritual healing for brokenness from past relationships
   - current relationships that need to be reconciled
   - current relationships that call for a demonstration of love by meeting needs
   - persons you sense God wants to love into the kingdom through your life

6. Ask each small-group member: *How can we pray for you this week?* Then take time to pray for each specific need or request.

Chapter Two

ℱHE 𝒢OSPEL ℳOVES
ℱHROUGH ℛELATIONSHIPS

Before I became a professor at Southwestern Seminary in Fort Worth, Texas, I preached and pastored churches for twenty-four years. Most of the concepts of evangelism I had read emphasized training Christians to tell strangers about the Lord. I call a stranger like this "Person X."

As I began to prepare to teach personal evangelism at the seminary, I did not take my position lightly. I was very aware of James's admonition, "Let not many of you become teachers, my brethren, knowing that as such we shall incur a stricter judgment" (James 3:1). So I realized, to whom much is given, much is required.

THE IMPORTANCE OF LIFESTYLE

Each year I teach more than one thousand students. Those students will literally go to the ends of the earth to carry the gospel. So I prayed, "Father, teach me first so that I may teach them." I didn't want to teach only concepts. My students didn't need head knowledge only. They needed to learn a lifestyle.

A person can never lead another closer to the Lord than he or she already is. Evangelism must flow from a life that is deeply in love with the Lord. It is not something you can learn in a textbook, take tests on, or make A's on to be assured of success. When you get out into the world, you will flunk the course if you do not have the right lifestyle. Your lifestyle should reveal what and who you really are.

Some are able evangelists in the pulpit who inspire many people to make decisions for the Lord. Yet, I have watched these same men act rudely toward a waitress or a salesperson and be first-class, carnal Christians. A Christian has no excuse for this. What does the world see in your daily life? Does the world see Jesus?

The essence of the walk in Jesus Christ is God's desire to produce his character within the Christian. If you are a Christian, you have a ministry, and that ministry will be wherever you are. As you go through life, God wants to reach the world around you. He wants to love your world through you and to draw it to him. If you let barriers hinder you from doing this, little else that you accomplish in life matters. Your life will be desperately empty.

A PATTERN IN THE NEW TESTAMENT

After recognizing the seriousness of the task before me in teaching evangelism to seminary students, the second thing I did was to commit myself to read through the New Testament once a month, looking for strategy. We are always looking for new types of plans. Everyone in education, every pastor is always looking for fresh, new ways of doing things. Variety is the spice of life. You do not want to do everything the same old way. But you want to do everything in a biblical way. How did the early Christians do evangelism in the New Testament?

As I studied the New Testament, I looked for a strategy, an idea. Finally, I began to see it rise like fog in the morning above a forest. At first, it was almost imperceptible. Then all at once, it became clear. It was there all the time! I just had not seen it. The most important word in the English language is *relationship*.

In the New Testament church, the gospel always moved on lines of relationship—to Jerusalem, Judea, Samaria, the uttermost parts of the earth—in waves that seemed to move outwardly. Have you ever thrown a rock in a pond and watched the waves move in all directions until they reached every edge of the pond? Well, that was the pattern I saw. The gospel of Jesus Christ began to spread through relationships in ever-growing circles.

If you read through the New Testament, you will see the centrality of relationship. It is nothing profound, but it is just as natural as anything can possibly be. If something is genuine in my life and your life, the natural thing to want to do is to share it with those we know. Isn't that reasonable to assume?

It seemed to me that we were always training people in evangelism to go to Person X out there somewhere. But there is no prior relationship established with Person X. Lifestyle evangelism in the New Testament did not begin with Person X. It worked through relationships that had already been established. Let's look at a few.

ANDREW AND SIMON PETER

At the beginning of his ministry, Jesus began to choose disciples to follow him. Andrew was the first. Notice what Andrew did when he first met Jesus:

> John [the Baptist] was standing with two of his disciples, and he looked upon Jesus as He walked, and said, "Behold, the Lamb of God!" And the two disciples heard him speak, and they followed Jesus. And Jesus turned, and beheld them following, and said to them, "What do you seek?" And they said to Him, "Rabbi (which translated means Teacher), where are You staying?" He said to them, "Come, and you will see." They came therefore and saw where He was staying; and they stayed with Him that day, for it was about the tenth hour. One of the two who heard John speak, and followed Him, was Andrew, Simon Peter's brother. He found first his own brother Simon, and said to him, "We have found the Messiah" (which translated means Christ). He brought him to Jesus. Jesus looked at him, and said, "You are Simon the son of John; you shall be called Cephas" (which is translated Peter) (John 1:35–42).

When Andrew met the Savior of the world, Jesus the Messiah, his first instinct was to introduce his brother Simon (later named Peter) to Jesus. Though we don't read very much about Andrew, his brother Peter became one of the great leaders of the early church, and he wrote two books of the New Testament. What a contribution Andrew made to the kingdom! He carried the gospel of Jesus Christ to one in his immediate family through a relationship.

PHILIP AND NATHANAEL

Jesus found another disciple from the same hometown as Andrew and Peter:

> The next day [Jesus] purposed to go forth into Galilee, and He found Philip. And Jesus said to him, "Follow Me." Now Philip was from Bethsaida, of the city of Andrew and Peter. Philip found Nathanael and said to him, "We have found Him of whom Moses in the Law and also the Prophets wrote, Jesus of Nazareth, the son of Joseph." And Nathanael said to him, "Can any good thing come out of Nazareth?" Philip said to him, "Come and

see." Jesus saw Nathanael coming to Him, and said of
him, "Behold, an Israelite indeed, in whom is no guile!"
Nathanael said to Him, "How do You know me?" Jesus
answered and said to him, "Before Philip called you, when
you were under the fig tree, I saw you." Nathanael
answered Him, "Rabbi, you are the Son of God; You are
the King of Israel." Jesus answered and said to him,
"Because I said to you that I saw you under the fig tree,
do you believe? You shall see greater things than these."
And He said to him, "Truly, truly, I say to you, You shall
see the heavens opened, and the angels of God ascending
and descending on the Son of Man" (John 1:43–51).

Philip met Jesus and responded to Jesus' invitation to follow him. He
then went to Nathanael and brought his friend to meet Jesus. When
Nathanael met Jesus, he acknowledged that Jesus must be the Son of God
and the King of Israel. Many believe that Nathanael is the same person
who is called Bartholomew in the other three gospels. These two friends
became two of the twelve disciples Jesus chose to be his closest compan-
ions. Philip carried the good news about Jesus through a relationship to
his friend, and both their lives were forever changed.

THE WOMAN AT THE WELL AND HER NEIGHBORS

Jesus took his disciples with him on a journey through Samaria—a
place that most Jews avoided because of prejudice. Beside the well at a
city named Sycar, Jesus introduced himself to a woman as the Christ
(Messiah) and as the "living water." She believed him and went immediately to share the good news with her neighbors:

So the woman left her waterpot, and went into the
city, and said to the men, "Come, see a man who told me
all the things that I have done; this is not the Christ, is
it?" They went out of the city, and were coming to Him.

And from that city many of the Samaritans believed in
Him because of the word of the woman who testified, "He
told me all the things that I have done." So when the
Samaritans came to Him, they were asking Him to stay
with them; and He stayed there two days. And many more
believed because of His word; and they were saying to the
woman, "It is no longer because of what you said that we
believe, for we have heard for ourselves and know that

this One is indeed the Savior of the world" (John 4:28–30, 39–42).

Here was a woman who probably was at the well at noon because she was not accepted by the other women who would normally draw water at the beginning or end of the day. She had been through five husbands and was living with a man she was not married to. When she realized that Jesus was the long-awaited Messiah, she hurried back to town to share the good news with her neighbors and relatives. After only two days with Jesus, many believed in him. One woman touched a whole city for Christ.

OTHERS

Throughout the New Testament, we have other examples of people who carried the gospel through relationships to others:

- Paul described to the Ephesian elders how he had proclaimed the message of Christ "publicly and from house to house" (Acts 20:20).
- When Cornelius (a Gentile) invited Peter (a Jew) to preach at his home, he invited all his household (probably including servants and family) to listen. These Gentiles believed Peter's message and the Holy Spirit came down on them all (Acts 10).
- Paul and Silas were in prison in Philippi singing hymns when an earthquake occurred. The jailer was ready to take his own life, when Paul and Silas intervened. They told him and all in his house about Jesus. Before the night was over, all the numbers of the household believed in Christ and were baptized (Acts 16:22–30).
- Jesus cast demons out of a wild man of the Gadarenes. After he healed the man, Jesus sent him away and told him: "'Return to your house and describe what great things God has done for you.' And he went away, proclaiming throughout the whole city what great things Jesus had done for him" (Luke 8:39).

EXPERIENCING THE PATTERN

I had been asked to teach an evangelism class for a couple of nights for a friend at a Bible institute. As I drove to class that first night, I kept mulling over this concept of relationship in my mind. When I got to the class, I continued to think through this concept, and I drew seven circles on the board. They were like a target with a bull's-eye in the center, *concentric circles*.

I said to the class, "The gospel moves on contiguous lines—on lines of relationship." I explained the circles and what each circle represents.

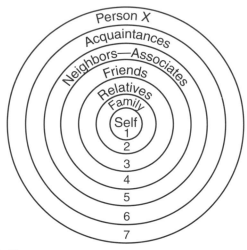

- Circle 1: Self
- Circle 2: Family
- Circle 3: Relatives
- Circle 4: Friends
- Circle 5: Neighbors and Associates
- Circle 6: Acquaintances
- Circle 7: Person X

"Now," I said, "I believe that God holds you responsible for everyone he brings into your sphere of influence. Many of us come to study evangelism to go from Circle 1 out to Circle 7 to salve our consciences because there are ruptured relationships in Circles 2 through 6 that we prefer to skip over.

"When we have ruptured relationships horizontally with people, we also have a ruptured relationship vertically with God. It is not that we do not know the Lord. It is just that he is not really Lord of our lives. We are not willing to let him be Lord of everything and accept, love, and forgive people on his conditions.

"With Person X, our lifestyles do not have to be consistent. We can talk to Person X and then be on our way. There is nothing wrong with telling Person X about Jesus. We are supposed to do that. God will bring many strangers into our lives. However, if we cannot tell people in Circles 2 through 6 about the Lord, we are hypocritical. We are play acting. We are unreal people. If our relationship with the Lord is genuine, we will want to share the good news of Christ with those closest to us."

RECONCILED AT HOME FIRST

As I spoke to that class, I noticed a lady sitting on the back row. I watched her face become distorted. She was hurting. She was either having a gall bladder attack, or I was saying something that was hurting her. It was the latter. She left very quickly that night, not knowing that she would have to put up with me again.

I came back the next week. She was not expecting me. She looked up and said, "Oh, you again!" That always warms a teacher's heart! She sat down and said, "I want to see you after class."

Wow! No one had talked to me like that since the second grade when I used to . . . I won't tell you what I did.

Afterward, she came to my desk and said, "You hurt me last week."

I said, "Dear heart, I do not understand."

"You said that I came here to study to tell Person X about the Lord." She had personalized it. She had internalized it. She continued, "You see, I was estranged from my husband and my two sons. It was not their fault. It was mine. I came here to salve my conscience. After last week, the Holy Spirit took hold of me. I knew I must go home."

As she wept, she said, "I want you to know that I have accepted Jesus Christ's conditions for reconciliation. You see, my conditions would never have reconciled us. I had to accept Jesus Christ's conditions."

Please understand this. You may accept another person's conditions or you may establish your own conditions for a relationship, but it will never be a lasting relationship until you accept Jesus Christ's conditions. Why? Because that is the way you are designed.

She wept and said, "I am back at home now. But do you know what has happened? The timidity that I always have had toward Person X is gone. When Jesus became Lord of my relationships, he took away my timidity."

I said, "Glory! That's it—*relationships!*"

"CLASS, WE'RE STARTING OVER"

I went back to my own class at the seminary the next day. My dear students never know what is going to happen next. I said, "Scratch everything; we are starting over." Well, we were halfway through the semester. They looked at me like a calf looks at a new gate.

I continued by saying, "Class, I have a new assignment. It is an assignment that you cannot finish this semester. You will not finish it until God takes you home."

I drew those concentric circles and said, "The gospel did not go from house to house to house to house down the street like a nice, neat census.

"It went from house to house to house to house."

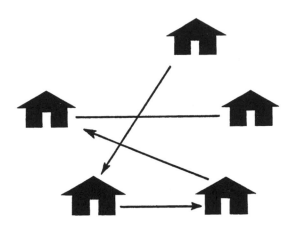

I continued, "God holds you responsible for every person who comes into your spheres of influence—into your concentric circles. There are people in all of your circles whom you touch every day, and you do not even see them. Some of them are cantankerous; some of them you do not like; and some of them you really do not want to love. But they are there in relationship to you. They are there for you to love—to meet their needs—so the Father can draw them to his Son Jesus.

"How many of you have loved ones whom you are not sure know the Lord? How many of you have come to seminary to learn only how to go and tell Person X about the Lord?"

RECONCILED TO AN ABSENTEE FATHER

Just as I was going to continue, a young man on my left blurted out, "Dr. Thompson, I have all kinds of problems with that!" I turned and said, "What's the matter, Jim?"

The impact of the moment had overwhelmed him. The assignment had touched an area of bitterness in his life that he did not know how to deal with. He said, "You do not understand! You grew up in a Christian home. But my father abandoned my mother and me twenty-six-and-a-half years ago. I am twenty-seven years old. I have never seen him. I do not want to see him!"

I whispered, "Oh." A class of sixty. He did not realize what had happened to him. All that pent-up anger just rolled out.

Gently, I turned to the board. Speaking silently to the Lord, I said, "Lord Jesus, love Jim through me. Please meet his need." A passage of Scripture came to mind. I wrote on the board Matthew 6:14–15. My translation was, "Because of the love of Jesus and his forgiveness in my life, I must be ready to forgive if I am to be forgiven."

I said, "In other words, you do not give people what they deserve. You give them what they need."

I turned back around, and the Holy Spirit was doing His work. I said, "Jim, I think that you are in this class through divine providence. I think God is going to teach me something and you something and this class something. For if I cannot forgive another on the grounds of God's infinite grace, then God is going to have great difficulty forgiving me (Matt. 6:14–15). Your father does not deserve forgiveness, but neither do you and neither do I."

Tears were trickling down Jim's cheeks. The Holy Spirit descended upon that class. Jim said, "What must I do? I do not know where my father is. He may not even be alive."

I said, "It does not matter. Your problem is one of attitude. You take it to God, let him tell you what to do, and leave it there. If God helps you find your father, you will know what to do."

Jim said, "Yes."

We called the class to prayer. It was a glorious time.

Weeks passed. One day Jim came sashaying into class about two feet off the ground. I thought he worked for Bell Helicopter. He said, "Dr. Thompson, I have something to say. I just have to share it. I cannot wait!"

Well, by that time I had lost my train of thought anyway. I said, "Say on!"

Jim said, "Last night I received two telephone calls. The first came from my mom saying that one of my godly aunts had gone to be with the Lord. I always thought that she was my mother's sister, but she was not. She was my father's sister who had stayed close to the family.

"At 11:00 I received a second call, and the voice on the other end said, 'Jim? Son? . . . although I have no right to call you son. I have heard that you are at Southwestern Seminary preparing for the ministry. I thought you would like to know that recently I gave my life to Jesus Christ. Can you forgive me for what I have done?'"

Jim said, "When I could quit sobbing, we talked. We spent an hour on the phone. My father said, 'Son, may I come to your graduation?'"

In May of that year, we were marching in the processional of the graduation exercise in all our academic regalia. Well, someone grabbed me out of the line. It was Jim.

He took me over to a little man who looked up through his trifocals. In tears, Jim said, "Dr. Thompson, this is my father. Dad, this is my professor."

What do you say? We just sort of went into a three-cornered hug. That, dear friend, is the gospel of Jesus Christ!

THE NEED FOR RIGHT RELATIONSHIPS

If there are ruptured relationships between you and those in your concentric circles, there is going to be a rupture of the flow of the Holy Spirit through your life. Jesus put it very plainly in Matthew: "If therefore you are presenting your offering at the altar, and there remember that your brother has something against you, leave your offering there before the altar, and go your way; first be reconciled to your brother, and then come and present your offering" (Matt. 5:23–24).

Jesus taught us to confess wrong relationships and make them right before coming to worship the Father. We must be reconciled with others to be right with God.

I believe with all my heart that when you have to dig deep into your spiritual well to get the Living Water flowing, there is something wrong in a relationship somewhere. When relationships are right, the flow of the Holy Spirit is like an artesian well that bursts up and out and over! All of our training for evangelism will be less useful than it can be until we make our wrong relationships right.

Personalizing Chapter 2

Using a journal or notebook, respond to the following questions or activities. Record details that will help you understand and apply the truths of this chapter to your own life.

1. Consider beginning a reading of the New Testament, especially the Gospels and Acts, to see for yourself the pattern of reaching out through relationships described in this chapter.
2. In your notebook or journal, begin to compile a list of people in your concentric circles of concern. We'll work on a more detailed survey later. Begin by listing the names of one or two people in each of the following concentric circles:
   • Circle 2: Family
   • Circle 3: Relatives
   • Circle 4: Friends
   • Circle 5: Neighbors and Associates (business, school, etc.)
   • Circle 6: Acquaintances
3. Look back over your list, and circle the names of those people who do not know Jesus Christ as their personal Savior. If you don't know, write a question mark beside the name.
4. Begin praying for the people whose names you just listed.
   • Ask the Lord to show you any broken relationship that needs mending. If he reveals one, begin praying about how to be reconciled in that relationship.
   • Ask the Lord to make you a channel of his love to these people.
   • Ask the Lord to give you a sensitivity to their needs.
   • For those who do not know Jesus Christ as their Savior, ask God to begin engineering circumstances in their lives to draw them to himself.

Building Up the Body

Use the following questions and activities with your small group to help one another apply these truths to your lives and to build up the body of Christ.

1. Discuss examples from your own experiences of how a Christian's lifestyle has had a positive or negative influence on others coming to Christ.
2. Invite volunteers to tell how they came to a saving relationship with Jesus Christ. Who was the person most responsible for helping you come to Christ, and what was that person's relationship to you?

3. How have you experienced God working through a relationship to bring a person to faith in Christ?

4. Take a few moments to pray. Ask God to identify for each group member one person in his or her concentric circles who needs to know Christ as Savior. After praying, invite members to identify the person on their "Most Wanted" list. Pray for each other and for those who need the Lord.

5. Ask each small-group member: *How can we pray for you this week?* Then take time to pray for those specific needs or requests.

Chapter Three

A STRATEGY FOR REACHING YOUR WORLD

BEING AN AMBASSADOR FOR CHRIST

Religion is good views about God. But the gospel is good news from God. Reformation is man's doing. Transformation is God's doing. When the Holy Spirit sheds the love of God in our hearts, he puts his ministry of love into action in and through our lives.

As a Christian, what should be the theme of your life? What should you be as God's servant? Paul answered this question in part in his letter to the Corinthians:

> Therefore if any man is in Christ, he is a new creature; the old things passed away; behold, new things have come. Now all these things are from God, who reconciled us to Himself through Christ, and gave us the ministry of reconciliation, namely, that God was in Christ reconciling the world to Himself, not counting their trespasses against them, and He has committed to us the word of reconciliation. Therefore, we are ambassadors for Christ, as though God were entreating through us; we beg you on behalf of Christ, be reconciled to God. He made Him who knew no sin to be sin on our behalf, that we might become the righteousness of God in Him (2 Cor. 5:17–21).

These verses are the gospel in a nutshell. They tell how God brought us to himself through Christ's death on the cross to pay for our sin. They reveal how we are responsible for sharing the good news of how he reconciled us and how he wants us to reconcile others, through Christ to himself. As we saw in the last chapter, God intended that gospel to spread across the relationships his people had with others in their circles of influence.

We are to share compassionately the good news of Jesus with lost people in the power of the Holy Spirit for the purpose of winning them to Jesus Christ as their Savior and Lord. They, in turn, will share him with others. This sharing is both the ministry and the word of reconciliation. Thus, God calls us to be ambassadors for Christ.

WHAT IS AN AMBASSADOR?

An ambassador is someone who represents someone other than himself at the court of another. My beloved friend, if you are a Christian, you are an ambassador of Jesus Christ. This should be the biblical motif with which you approach your lifestyle.

Wherever you go, you represent Jesus. At the office, you are an ambassador for Christ. Teaching school, running a business, buying your groceries, wherever, you are an ambassador for Christ. You represent the person of Jesus Christ everywhere you go.

Have you ever seen a "Christian" who by his attitudes of selfishness, unthoughtfulness, and self-centeredness did not represent Christ well? How tragic! Christians represent Jesus in every area of living. Wherever Christians go, twenty-four hours a day, we are ambassadors for Jesus Christ. As an ambassador, you are to plead with others to be reconciled (to get right) with God.

WHEN SHOULD YOUR MINISTRY BEGIN?

Some people have the wrong idea about Christian ministry. They say that when they learn something or grow to a certain point, they will begin ministry. I have students who say, "When I graduate and my ministry begins . . ." No! Your ministry is today. Do not waste a minute. God takes you where you are, and you are to begin your ministry now.

You will not have a ministry in the future if you do not have it now. If you will be faithful over a few things, God will make you ruler over many (Matt. 25:23). So, remember that your ministry is not out there somewhere in the future; it is now! The moment Jesus comes into your heart, your ministry begins. He wants to be free to work through you.

THE HIGHEST CALLING

The highest calling in the world is not to preach the gospel. The highest calling in the world is to be a Christian. Consequently, every one of us, in the reality of the word, is a minister and has a ministry within his or her own concentric circles.

Many people say, "God just did not intend for me to be a super Christian." That is right! He did not intend for you to be a super anything. He expects you to be you, in whom he dwells and fills.

"If I become a Spirit-filled Christian," many Christians say, "I will have to be a missionary or preacher or do something special." No! Some of the greatest Spirit-filled Christians I know sell parts in a hardware store, own businesses, teach in schools, or sell houses. They never preach a sermon, per se; they live one every day.

Being filled with the Spirit does not change a person from being an introvert into an extrovert. Many people think they should have some kind of personality change, but Jesus does not want to reproduce his personality in you. He wants to use your personality and reproduce his character in your personality. He wants to take you and reproduce his life in you. Then he wants to work through your life to reconcile a lost world to himself.

REACHING YOUR WORLD

Friends, we can devise many different plans to win the world to Jesus, and that is as it should be. That is how it had better be. You see, Jesus has commanded us to go and make disciples of the whole world: "Go therefore and make disciples of all the nations, baptizing them in the name of the Father and the Son and the Holy Spirit, teaching them to observe all that I commanded you; and lo, I am with you always, even to the end of the age" (Matt. 28:19–20).

I am not talking about global evangelism; I am talking about your evangelism. I believe the Father's plan is for each of us to have a specific strategy to reach our world, and say, "This is my world, Father, and I am going to take it!" Then the Spirit of God will fall on us and fill us and speak to us, by us, and through us—"Lord, as long as you leave me in this clay house, I will take my world."

Fortunately, God doesn't expect us to reach our world alone. Jesus said, "You shall receive power when the Holy Spirit has come upon you; and you shall be My witnesses both in Jerusalem, and in all Judea and Samaria, and even to the remotest part of the earth" (Acts 1:8). So, every believer has his Jerusalem. You will find yours in your concentric circles. You have a Judea. Your Judea is not like anyone else's Judea. You have a Samaria. The Jews did not like the Samaritans, and you probably have people in your Samaria you do not like. But you do not have to like them to love them. In effect, God says, "You meet the needs of those Samaritans; whatever they are, you meet them." You also have an uttermost part of the earth that God will draw into your circles.

SEVEN STAGES FOR MAKING DISCIPLES

God wants to work through your life to make disciples of those in your world—in your concentric circles. He is so creative that he can do work in any way he chooses. He will work through your life in unique ways that you will not learn from reading a book like this. I can, however, share with you some actions that will contribute to the ways God can and will work through your life.

I've identified seven stages for making disciples. In the following diagram, you can see how these seven stages encircle the concentric circles. These stages apply for every one of those circles as you seek to join God in making disciples of those who need Jesus Christ.

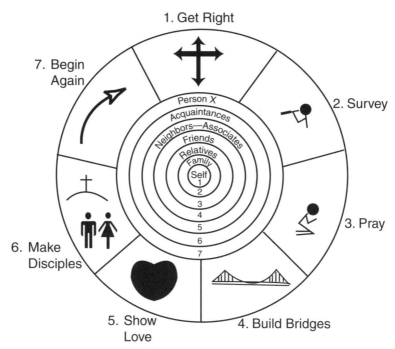

Seven Stages for Making Disciples
Stage 1: Get Right—Get right with God, self, and others.
Stage 2: Survey—Survey your relationships.
Stage 3: Pray—Work with God through prayer.

Stage 4: Build Bridges—Build relationship bridges to people.
Stage 5: 'Show Love—Show God's love by meeting needs.
Stage 6: Make Disciples—Make disciples and help them grow.
Stage 7: Begin Again—Help new Christians make disciples.

Let me overview the seven stages for you, and then we will look at each one in more detail through the remainder of the book.

STAGE 1: GET RIGHT—GET RIGHT WITH GOD, SELF, AND OTHERS

The beginning place for everything is a right relationship with God. First you must come to God on his conditions for forgiveness and salvation. When you make Christ Lord of your life, you forever surrender the right to choose whom you will love. He will begin to guide your life to be on mission with him. If you have not been in a right and obedient relationship with God since your salvation, you need to repent and get back into that right relationship with him so his Spirit can flow through your life.

You also need to have a proper view of yourself. We are commanded to love others as we love ourselves. You need to love yourself and understand who you are in Christ. A right relationship with Christ can bring balance to your life that will not only make life more meaningful and fulfilling for you, but it will also be far more effective in revealing the character of Christ to others.

Once you have a right vertical relationship with your heavenly Father and a balanced view of self, God moves you to correct relationships with others. You cannot be right with God and still have broken relationships with others. Reconciled relationships with others will clean the channel in your life so that the love of God can flow through you to others around you. The gospel will move through these right relationships.

STAGE 2: SURVEY—SURVEY YOUR RELATIONSHIPS

Many people who have been Christians for a long time may not think they have relationships with people who are lost. We don't stop to think about all the people that God brings into our lives or into the circles of our influence. I've found that when people begin to identify the people in their concentric circles in a survey, they find all kinds of people who need the Lord.

One of my youth directors told me that his teenagers kept saying, "We know a few kids at school, but we really do not know many people who do not know the Lord." He shared the principles of concentric circles with forty of these young people on a retreat. Then he gave them six sheets of paper each and two hours alone to pray and make their surveys. They came back with nineteen hundred names. Several have already been won to the Lord. That is why we will help you survey the people God has placed in your concentric circles.

I will guide you in identifying people in your circles of influence and in recording basic information that can guide your praying, bridge building, and loving. First we'll look at those closest to you in your immediate family and your circle of relatives. Then we'll start identifying your friends, neighbors, business or school associates, and acquaintances. I will also help you think about the "Person X" people that God may bring across your path. This survey will become a prayer list for you to begin praying for those whom God has brought into your concentric circles.

STAGE 3: PRAY—WORK WITH GOD THROUGH PRAYER

Prayer is not just a religious activity you go through before you begin your work for the Lord. Prayer is a relationship with the Master of the universe. When you pray, you enter the throne room of heaven where the decisions that govern the universe are made. God invites us to pray so that when he answers, we will know he did it. He will get the glory.

I will help you learn to pray for wisdom and discernment as you seek to make disciples. You will learn to pray that God engineer circumstances in the lives of others to draw them to himself and to his Son Jesus Christ. You will pray about the people in your survey and watch to see where God is working in their lives. When you become aware of needs, that will be your invitation to join God and show his love to the needy person.

STAGE 4: BUILD BRIDGES—BUILD RELATIONSHIP BRIDGES TO PEOPLE

Sometimes your relationships with people in your concentric circles is so shallow or distant that you have little way of reaching out to the person in love. At other times you will become aware of a person who needs the Lord, and you will intentionally begin building a relationship bridge to that person so that God's love can flow to him or her.

You can build relationship bridges to people in a variety of ways. You can show an interest in them during special times of joy or times of stress. You can build bridges through shared interests or hobbies. You will find that building bridges is not a waste of time. When people come to Christ through existing relationships with Christians, they are far more likely to follow through in establishing a growing relationship with a church— probably your church.

Stage 5: Show Love—Show God's Love by Meeting Needs

One of the best ways to be used by God in reaching your world is by showing God's love. Love is meeting needs. As God engineers circumstances in the lives of those you are praying for, he will create an opportunity for the person to experience his love through your life. As he loves the person through you by meeting his or her needs, he will begin drawing that person to his Son.

God engineers the circumstances for you to show his love. God works in your heart to motivate you to love a person who may not be very lovely. God also provides the resources to meet the needs of others through you. When you allow God's love to flow through you, your life becomes a channel of God's love, and people will experience God's love through you. They will know they have been loved by a heavenly Father, and they will begin to sense his invitation to become a part of his family by adoption and by the saving grace of his Son.

Stage 6: Make Disciples—Make Disciples and Help Them Grow

As you continue to pray, cultivate relationships, and show God's love, you will reach a point where you need to confront a person with the claims of Jesus Christ on his or her life. When you see other people as God sees them—helplessly lost without Christ—you will want to share with them the good news you know about Christ. You will point them to God and his conditions for salvation.

Your responsibility is to bear witness of the Christ who lives in you, to tell about your faith in him. The Holy Spirit is the one with the responsibility of bringing conviction of sin. He will convince the person of the truth of the gospel. When a person yields his or her life to Christ, you will be able to rejoice with the angels in heaven. You will experience the joy of being used by God to see a miracle happen in changing a life.

After people turn to Christ, they need to grow as his disciples. You will help them develop their personal relationship with Jesus through prayer and the Word of God. You will guide them to surrender to the authority of Christ so that he becomes their Lord. You will help them begin to develop the character of Christ as they die to self and allow him to live through them.

Stage 7: Begin Again—Help New Christians Make Disciples

Making disciples does not end with a decision to follow Christ. That is the beginning. Helping a new Christian grow into a fully devoted follower of Jesus Christ is also a part of the church's assignment in making disciples. The cycle of making disciples doesn't end when a person becomes a Christian. For that person, the cycle begins.

You will be able to help others get right with God, self, and others. You will help them survey, pray, and build bridges to the people in their concentric circles of concern. You can encourage them as they become channels of God's love. Then you will be able to rejoice with them when they see their loved ones, friends, and associates become disciples of Jesus Christ.

PERSONALIZING CHAPTER 3

Using a journal or notebook, respond to the following questions or activities. Record details that will help you understand and apply the truths of this chapter to your own life.

1. Read again 2 Corinthians 5:17–21. Describe in your own words what it means to you to be an ambassador for Christ.
2. When and how did you come to know that God has a ministry for your life that includes making disciples? How do you think God would grade your faithfulness to that ministry thus far?
3. In your notebook or journal, see if you can list the seven stages for making disciples (Begin Again; Build Bridges; Get Right; Make Disciples; Pray; Show Love; Survey) in their proper order. Then check your work.
4. Based on these brief descriptions, which one or two stages do you sense will be the greatest challenges for you to apply in your concentric circles? Which one (if any) do you sense God already has especially gifted and prepared you for?
5. Pray that God will guide you and gift you to join him in his work of making disciples of the lost people in your concentric circles. Accept his calling as an ambassador, and pledge your allegiance to him as your king. Talk to him about any concerns you may have about making disciples through your relationships.

BUILDING UP THE BODY

Use the following questions and activities with your small group to help one another apply these truths to your lives and to build up the body of Christ.

1. Discuss what being an ambassador for Christ means. Invite volunteers to describe people they have known who were effective ambassadors for Christ.

2. Why should a Christian have a personal strategy for reaching his or her world?

3. Take turns reviewing the seven stages for making disciples. Invite volunteers to identify the stage(s) that they sense will be most difficult to apply.

4. What have you done or experienced in the past week as a result of our study thus far? How is God working in your relationships?

5. What do you sense is the most meaningful or valuable truth God is teaching you about concentric circles or the seven stages for making disciples?

6. Ask each small-group member: *How can we pray for you this week?* Then take time to pray for those specific needs or requests.

Chapter Four

*T*HREE *B*ARRIERS TO *S*HARING THE *G*OSPEL

WHAT IS THE GOSPEL?

The meaning for the English word *gospel* is "good news." It is used seventy-six times in the New Testament. When you anglicize the Greek word, you have *euangelion*. Notice the "eu" on the front of the word. In Greek, *eu* always means good. *Euphonos* means good sound. *Eulogos* means good word. Actually, the Old English word was *godspel* if you look up *gospel* in *Webster's Third Unabridged Dictionary*. As *godspel* was translated, it became known as "gospel."

It only seems right that any good news we have, we would want to share with those who are closest to us. These people are those with whom we have developed relationships.

Sometimes we Christians become artificial and, therefore, hypocritical. We want to carry the good news out to Person X somewhere, but we do not want to carry it to the ones around us. You may say, "But it is hard to witness to people I really know." If what you say is true, the relationships you have are not real. In reality, your love and concern for yourself is greater than your love for those closest to you. So let's look at three barriers that can keep us from sharing the good news in our concentric circles. A barrier is anything in your lifestyle that hinders you from sharing the gospel with another.

BARRIER #1: NOT KNOWING JESUS PERSONALLY

The first and foremost barrier hindering you from reaching out to love people in your concentric circles is that perhaps you have never met the One who is love. Have you met Jesus? The beginning place to be

37

prepared to share the good news with others is a right relationship with Jesus Christ. You must first get right with God.

With our five senses we perceive the world. We lock into our minds as knowledge what our five senses tell us. We can know about God mentally. Consequently, many people only know *about* God. They can give many concepts *about* God, but they do not know God by experience.

My *body* makes me world-conscious; my *mind* makes me self-conscious; and my *spirit* makes me God-conscious. But if my spirit is dead in trespasses and sin, a holy God cannot be there. I still have a spirit, but it is dead toward God. In the new birth, God breaks through and comes to dwell in me and makes me alive spiritually. I am then born from above.

The authority of the Christian life is no longer physical. When a Christian is born from above, the Spirit of God dwells in that person's spirit, flows through his mind, and moves through his body. Then we Christians, "present [our] bodies a living and holy sacrifice" (Rom. 12:1). Why?

So that "from his innermost being shall flow rivers of living water" (John 7:38). To what?

You are the channel through which the Holy Spirit wants to move and manifest himself to the world, and that happens when a person is born again. He or she is alive to God.

Perhaps you have deep needs in your own life. You are hurting. Remember that because God loves you, there is not a need in your life that he has not already made provision for. The greatest provision is that your sins be forgiven. You can join the church, lead a good moral life, help people, and give money to the church. But these actions cannot take away your sin.

Jesus Christ entered history and died to save us from our sins. He paid the price of death for our sins so that we can be forgiven. Jesus' death is God's provision for our need. Because of him, we have eternal life. Everything has been done that is required for you to get right with God. You have to come to God on his conditions. If you have never done that yourself, you will not be able to witness about the good news that Jesus saves.

BARRIER #2: FEAR

Once you have gotten right with God, you need to get right with self. When self is all that God created it to be, Jesus will be able to manifest his life through you in power. If you don't get right with self, you will be shaky in your relationships with others.

A second barrier in sharing the good news with those we know is fear of rejection or fear of failure. Without a confident relationship with Christ and a right perspective of who we are in Christ, we will tend to be fearful of what others think and do. In order to understand fear, we need to see what God's Word says about it. In 2 Timothy 1:7 we find that fear does not come from God: "For God has not given us a spirit of timidity [fear], but of power and love and discipline."

We are also given a command to witness without fear: "But sanctify Christ as Lord in your hearts, always being ready to make a defense to everyone who asks you to give an account for the hope that is in you, yet with gentleness and reverence; and keep a good conscience so that in the thing in which you are slandered, those who revile your good behavior in Christ may be put to shame" (1 Pet. 3:15–16).

HARVARD UNIVERSITY

Because of my work with cancer patients and my ministry to people in working with stress, I had the opportunity to lecture on stress in the department of psychology at Harvard. This is what I told the audience: "I am by trade an academician, but this morning I do not want to be an academician. I just want to invite you into my own vulnerability, into my own experience with cancer. I want to tell you my story. My purpose for being here is not to come up with a scientific treatise but to meet needs in your life . . . in other words, I want to love you."

I continued, "I want to love you, and I want to meet needs in your life. Someone in your family, or someone that you touch, or perhaps even you, may someday have cancer." Then I told them about the person of Jesus Christ as the center of life, how he has designed us, and how stress affects the human body.

After I spoke, a number of people lined up to speak to me. Many said, "We have not heard this about the person of Christ." You see, most intellectuals have never heard a clear presentation of the gospel, the real story about Jesus Christ. So, do not be intimidated by people in the academic or the secular world. They hurt just like everybody else. Go ahead and love them. Do not be concerned about what they think of you. You do not have to be fearful; you're an ambassador for the King.

AGREE WITH GOD AND OBEY

To hear something is one thing; to apply it is another. When God gives us insight into himself and his will, he holds us responsible for what he teaches us. If he gives us a truth about himself and we do not obey it, we are hurt spiritually. One of my students honestly admitted, "Then I just want to be ignorant."

But that student's choice is not the answer either. We need to claim 2 Timothy 1:7 and agree with God. We need to step forward and be obedient without being intimidated. "He who has My commandments and keeps them, he it is who loves Me; and he who loves Me shall be loved by My Father, and I will love him, and will disclose Myself to him" (John 14:21).

If you agree with what God has told you about what he wants you to do and you obey it, God has said he will disclose or make himself conspicuous or real in your life. When Jesus reveals his will for your life and you obey him, he becomes conspicuous. He becomes real.

The times in my life when Jesus has been most real have been those times when I have, out of sheer obedience, said, "Father, I do not know how, why, or what, but I will obey you."

I cannot measure obedience to God on a slide rule. I do not plan to put it in some theory. I am just saying that it is God's nature to become conspicuous or real in our lives if we obey him. You need to agree with God that fear does not come from him. Then trust him to give you the "spirit of power and love and discipline."

BUILDING YOUR HOUSE ON A ROCK

In Matthew 7:24–27 Jesus said that the one who hears and obeys his word is like a man who built his house on a rock. When the storms of life come, the house will stand. When you obey God's word about witnessing without fear, Jesus keeps his promise of making himself conspicuous in your life.

I will never forget when the seminary invited me to teach, and Carolyn and I moved to Fort Worth. Soon after, we decided to build our own home. We designed it, selected our lot, and began to build. The Lord said to build your house upon a rock, and I did. With grubbing hoe and pick, one of my dear students and I began to dig the foundation.

One day, leaning on the pick and perspiring, that student said to me as we labored together, "Doc, I am really glad about one thing."

"What?" I asked.

"I am glad you did not decide to build a basement."

One night we were working late to finish digging the pit for the fireplace. The house has two stories and stacked fireplaces: one in the family room and one in our master bedroom upstairs. We had to dig down five feet into the rock to put in enough concrete and steel to support the weight of a double fireplace.

Well, that cold windy night, dressed in an old trench coat and hard hat, I dug while Carolyn held the light. A police officer, new on the beat, stopped his car, beamed his light on us, rolled down his window, and yelled, "What are you doing?"

Carolyn looked at me, and I shouted back to him, "Digging a grave!"

You talk about getting attention. The officer jumped out of his car to have a look as we explained the situation. We became friends. He stopped each night to check on our progress.

Later that night we finally went to the house we were renting. We went straight to bed. I was exhausted. Carolyn had already collapsed, and the house was very, very still. All of a sudden, I heard the drip of a faucet.

If I will be really still, maybe Carolyn will hear it and get up and turn it off, I thought.

Well, she did not. Instead, I felt a gentle, little hand touch me and say, "Honey, please turn off the faucet." I want to tell you something, friend. That dripping water was the most conspicuous thing in the room. I could not divert my attention from it.

When we pray, "Father, I want you to be conspicuous; I want to sense your presence," God will be as real to us as that dripping faucet was to me. As you walk through each day of your life, Jesus wants to be conspicuous. He wants to be so conspicuous that you cannot ignore him or make any decision without him. That is how conspicuous and real Jesus wants to be in every Christian's life. As you obey him, he will be reflected in power and love and discipline, not in timidity and fear.

BARRIER #3: BROKEN RELATIONSHIPS

Finally, we can be right with God and self but have broken relationships with those around us. Ruptured relationships hinder the movement of the Spirit of God within Christians' lives. They neutralize our witness and its importance. Broken relationships shut off the divine well that can flow to all our world. To keep the divine well flowing, we Christians need to right all broken relationships.

Because of broken relationships, your conscience may not be clear. You may feel guilty over an offense, or you may feel like a hypocrite asking a person to be reconciled to God when you cannot get reconciled with another person. Right any broken relationships you may have. Do whatever is necessary to clear your conscience by making any wrongs right. Then the Holy Spirit can have a clear channel through which to flow. You need to get right with others in order to be prepared to share the gospel through your concentric circles.

PERSONALIZING CHAPTER 4

Using a journal or notebook, respond to the following questions or activities. Record details that will help you understand and apply the truths of this chapter to your own life.

1. How would you evaluate your vertical relationship with God?
   a. I really don't have much of a relationship with God.
   b. I don't have the faith relationship with Jesus Christ you described in this chapter, but I would like to come to know him that way.
   c. I do have that faith relationship with Jesus Christ, but I've strayed from closeness with him. I need to repent of sin and return to him.
   d. I do have a faith relationship with Jesus Christ and seek daily to walk in a right relationship with him.
2. If you were asked to explain the gospel or good news about salvation through Jesus Christ, what would you say based on your personal experience? What Scriptures would you use?
3. Describe a time you hesitated to share your faith with someone because of fear. What was the reason for your fear?
4. If you had a close Christian friend who was afraid to share Christ with a family member, what would you tell him or her to help overcome the fear?
5. What relationships, if any, has God identified that are broken and need to be reconciled? What have you already done to begin getting those relationships right?
6. As you pray today, identify any hindrances or barriers you have sensed that may keep you from sharing the gospel effectively. Ask God to teach you, guide you, correct you, and encourage you to be an effective witness for him.

BUILDING UP THE BODY

Use the following questions and activities with your small group to help one another apply these truths to your lives and to build up the body of Christ.

1. Based upon your experiences, what are the greatest barriers to your sharing the gospel with others? How have you experienced God's help in overcoming those barriers? What Scriptures have guided, corrected, or encouraged you to overcome those barriers?

2. Which of the three barriers in this chapter do you sense is the greatest barrier to the sharing of the gospel by members of your church? What do you sense God might want you to do to help remove that barrier so that the gospel will flow freely through your members to the lost world?

3. What, if anything, do you sense God is doing to reconcile relationships in your concentric circles? How are you experiencing his healing and victory in restored relationships?

4. What have you done or experienced in the past week as a result of our study thus far? How is God working in your relationships?

5. Ask each small-group member: *How can we pray for you this week?* Then take time to pray for those specific needs or requests.

Stage 1

Get Right:
Get Right with God,
Self, and Others

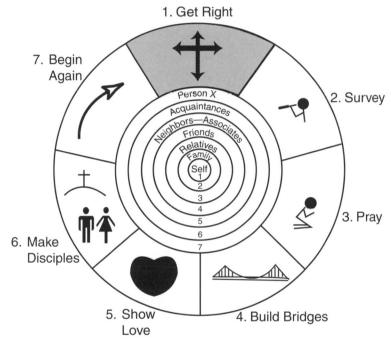

STAGE 1 SUMMARY

GET RIGHT WITH GOD, SELF, AND OTHERS

The beginning place for everything is a right relationship with God. First you must come to God on his conditions for forgiveness and salvation. When you make Christ Lord of your life, you forever surrender the right to choose whom you will love. He will begin to guide your life to be on mission with him. If you have not been in a right and obedient relationship with God since your salvation, you need to repent and get back into that right relationship with him so his Spirit can flow through your life.

You also need to have a proper view of yourself. We are commanded to love others as we love ourselves. You need to love yourself and understand who you are in Christ. A right relationship with Christ can bring balance to your life that will not only make life more meaningful and fulfilling for you, but it will also be far more effective in revealing the character of Christ to others.

Once you have a right vertical relationship with your heavenly Father and a balanced view of self, God moves you to correct relationships with others. You cannot be right with God and still have broken relationships with others. Reconciled relationships with others will clean the channel in your life so that the love of God can flow through you to others around you. The gospel will move through these right relationships.

Chapter Five

*G*ET *R*IGHT WITH *G*OD

In the last chapter, I mentioned three barriers that can hinder you from sharing the gospel with others. Until you overcome those barriers, you will be limited in your ability to be used by God to make disciples of others. Stage 1 is the place to begin overcoming any barriers in your life that might hinder your witness. You need to get into a right relationship with God, with self, and with others. In this chapter, we're going to focus on that first and most important relationship—your relationship with God.

A HOLLYWOOD PRODUCER

I boarded a plane bound for San Francisco one December and found my seat. Sitting on my left was a professor from the University of Texas, a deacon from one of the churches in Austin and a delightful fellow. We talked for a few moments.

On my right was a man who seemed very busy trying to get some writing done. I did not bother him. He was a Hollywood producer. We just greeted each other. I knew I had three hours with him. He was not going anywhere, not for three hours anyway. After a time he put his pen down, and we began talking. He asked, "What do you do?" I long since have learned not to tell people I am a Baptist preacher, especially if I am on a three-hour flight. They may just have a horror spell right there and jump!

Instead, I replied, "Well, I am a teacher." Then I waited.

He asked, "What do you teach?" Do you want me to say that I told him I teach evangelism at a theological seminary? No! I was not going to do that either.

"That is interesting you should ask," I continued. "What I basically teach is that the most important word in the English language is *relation-ship*. If we can solve the relationship problems in this world, we have

47

solved domestic problems, neighbor problems, city problems, and international problems."

Well, he looked out the window and thought for a moment, and then he said, "Hey, that is right!" Then I picked up a copy of *Time* and started reading. But he persisted, "Is that all you are going to tell me?"

"You want to know more?" And so I began. I said to him exactly what I am going to explain to you in this book. I explained that there are two types of relationships: horizontal relationships with people; and the vertical relationship with the Creator of the universe who has laid down the basis for all of our other relationships. We are made by his design. If we follow his design, things work. If we do not follow his design, things do not work. Because man basically has not followed God's design, relationships are not working very well.

Fortunately for us, however, God has also given us a plan to establish those right relationships. I told the man on the plane, "It is best seen in the teaching of Jesus Christ."

"Oh!" he said, "I have read the Bible. I agree with many things that Jesus said. Now, I do not believe everything the Bible says, but . . ."

"Well, that is what I teach." If I had been flying to Houston, which is only a forty-five-minute flight, I would not have been so free with my time. But this was a three-hour flight. I went back to reading *Time*. And he just sort of hung there. I read for a while.

"Tell me some more," the producer said.

I thought to myself, *Glad you asked.* Well, to make a long story short, we talked for a long time during that flight. The man had many problems with the Scriptures. But you and I know that many people in the secular world have rejected the Scriptures because they have heard only a caricature, not because they know anything about them.

I maintain that most people have not rejected Jesus Christ. They merely reject a caricature of him. They have rejected "churchianity." But they have not basically rejected Jesus Christ because they have never really heard about him. That is the tragedy. The producer and I talked about that; then we talked about the person of Jesus Christ.

"Well, how do you know who he is and what he is?" the man asked.

I went through the simple answer that Jesus either was who he said he was or he was psychotic or he was a great fraud. "Dick," I said, "you are going to have to decide ultimately who he is on the basis of the evidence. You cannot just conclude that Jesus was the greatest teacher that ever lived. You see, this great teacher said, 'I am God.' And no great teacher is a falsifier. You are either going to have to take Jesus at his word or reject him." Then I went back to reading *Time*.

My deacon friend in the next seat was praying for me. Finally, as we flew over El Capitan, the captain said, "There is Yosemite." We looked out, and I knew that time was running out.

I really began to pray. "Father, oh, Father, I cannot convince this fellow." He was having all kinds of trouble in relationships with his workers as well as with his family. He was trying to get his family back together and was frantic.

The latter part of that flight, as we crossed the mountains before circling the bay area, I saw tears forming in his eyes as he looked out the window. Then he turned to me and said, "Oscar, this morning I got down on my knees in a motel room in Dallas. I prayed, 'Dear God, if there is a God, I have to have help. Please send somebody.'" He reached over and took me by my elbow and said, "God sent you. Now what do I do?"

"The first thing that you are going to have to do is surrender to the absolute authority of Jesus Christ and let him be the master of your life. You are going to have to accept his conditions for coming to God. You cannot come on your own conditions.

"Dick, if you read the biography of every great Christian in history, you will find something very interesting. George Whitefield, John Wesley, Martin Luther, many great Christians whom history says were great men of God intensely struggled with God as they searched for him. All of them had one basic problem. Though they were seeking God with all their hearts, they were seeking him on their conditions. Only when they abandoned their conditions in coming to God did he accept them. When each one finally gave up and said, 'I will accept your conditions, whatever they are and whatever they cost me,' then instantly, immediately, God revealed himself."

As Dick got off the plane, he looked over and said, "Thank you, Oscar. I have needed this all my life."

THE VERTICAL RELATIONSHIP

There are two basic types of relationships in life. One, of course, is the vertical relationship you have with God. The other is the horizontal relationships you have with other people. When you establish by faith the proper vertical relationship with God as your heavenly Father, you are then able to have right horizontal relationships with others and deal with the basic problems of the world.

Dear reader, I do not know who you are, but I want you to know that the first step, the very first step in coming to know God intimately in a personal relationship, is coming to him on his conditions. I assume that you have already come into a saving relationship with Jesus Christ, but often that is a faulty assumption. If you have not come into that saving relationship, that is the first step for you in getting right with God.

The following Scriptures speak about our need and God's provision for salvation. Review these Scriptures and pray. Make sure that you have experienced God's saving grace in your life.

- All have sinned: "All have sinned and fall short of the glory of God" (Rom. 3:23).
- All deserve death: "For the wages of sin is death" (Rom. 6:23a).
- God provided for our salvation because of love: "God so loved the world, that He gave His only begotten Son, that whoever believes in Him should not perish, but have eternal life" (John 3:16).
- Christ paid our death penalty for us: "God demonstrates His own love toward us, in that while we were yet sinners, Christ died for us. Much more then, having now been justified by His blood, we shall be saved from the wrath of God through Him" (Rom. 5:8–9).
- Salvation is a free gift: "The free gift of God is eternal life in Christ Jesus our Lord" (Rom. 6:23b).
- Salvation is based on faith, not works: "By grace you have been saved through faith; and that not of yourselves, it is the gift of God; not as a result of works, that no one should boast" (Eph. 2:8–9).
- We receive the gift by confessing and believing: "If you confess with your mouth Jesus as Lord, and believe in your heart that God raised Him from the dead, you shall be saved; for with the heart man believes, resulting in righteousness, and with the mouth he confesses, resulting in salvation" (Rom. 10:9–10).
- God saves those who ask: "'WHOEVER WILL CALL UPON THE NAME OF THE LORD WILL BE SAVED'" (Rom. 10:13).
- Those who are saved are no longer condemned to death: "There is therefore now no condemnation for those who are in Christ Jesus" (Rom. 8:1).

A DAILY RELATIONSHIP

You receive God's grace when you come to him under his conditions. As a believer, you have to continue accepting those conditions every day. Colossians 2:6 says, "As you therefore have received Christ Jesus the

Lord, so walk in Him." Now what does that mean? It means that as you have accepted Jesus Christ by faith, you walk with him each day by faith.

Now, Amos 3:3 asked, "Can two walk together, except they be agreed?" (KJV). If "they be agreed," you have to come back and accept God's conditions in total agreement with him for the unfolding of that walk. Then, if you do that, the Lord says, "I will reveal Myself in your life." If you are not living in agreement with God and in obedience to him, you need to get right with God there also.

WALKING IN OBEDIENCE

Many people lose the joy of their salvation because they do not walk in obedience to the Lord. Barriers form, and they let those barriers defeat them. Do you want Jesus to be real to you? Write down John 14:21 and commit it to memory: "He who has My commandments and keeps them, he it is who loves Me; and he who loves Me shall be loved by My Father, and I will love him, and will disclose Myself to him" (John 14:21).

Jesus was saying here that he will make himself real. Now I want to show you something more. Your search for Jesus is not self-disclosure. He reveals himself. He makes himself real. Do you want Jesus to be real to you? Then obey him. The times in your life when Jesus was real were the times when you faced a major decision and decided to do it his way. You must say, "Father, I do not care what it costs. I do not care what I have to do." The man who walks with God every day has the reality of his presence as God manifests himself. This is God's promise, as recorded in John 14:21.

One of God's commands is to "go therefore and make disciples of all nations" (Matt. 28:19). One denomination may say, "Well, if we baptize a hundred thousand more next year than we did this year, we will rejoice." But this is no criterion, since God's criterion is to "make disciples of all nations." But, you are only responsible for everybody in your concentric circles. Why? Because God has enough grace to save all of them and meet all of their needs. All you have to do is be faithful and available.

God is alive and well in you, but is he in control? Are there barriers you have not overcome? Is he free to do all he wants to do in your life? Are you obedient to him? John 14:21 says that if you are obedient, he will make himself real to you.

Jesus needs to be real in your life. If he is not as real as he used to be, perhaps you need to go back and check the original problem—obedience. What did he tell you to do? When did you last disobey him?

51

Perhaps the problem of disobedience comes because of a ruptured relationship. Jesus said, "If you forgive men for their transgressions, your heavenly Father will also forgive you. But if you do not forgive men, then your Father will not forgive your transgressions" (Matt. 6:14–15). God laid down the law here about ruptured relationships. We do not grieve over them. We just move.

I tell my young preachers that the problem with some of us is that we go out into a church and immediately rupture a relationship somewhere. Because we have so much pride, we will not admit we are wrong. Perhaps the other person was wrong, but we are to be the initiators of reconciliation.

If we allow our pride to run rampant, along will come another rupture and another. Eventually, as a result of all these ruptured relationships with people around us, we do not pastor anymore. We rupture enough relationships so that we have to move to another church. Then the cycle starts all over again. When will we learn that we are to be the initiators of reconciliation because God is the initiator of reconciliation?

Take an inventory of your life. You will find that your happiest days were those days of good relationships; the days of agony were those days of broken relationships.

You see, your relationships can make you the happiest person in the world or they can make you miserable and devastated. Why? The answer is that God has made us to have relationships.

WHAT REALLY MAKES YOU HAPPY?

Things do not make you happy, although the world has bought the concept that they do. Things may excite you for a moment, but they will not make you happy. Then what does make you happy? Think back to chapter 1. That which satisfies the deepest longing of your being is a relationship with someone.

But remember, when we build a relationship with someone, we do not build that relationship on our conditions. Our conditions are always changing. We must build relationships on God's conditions.

Relationships satisfy. They meet our needs. Have you ever seen a lonely person? Have you ever been lonely? Have you ever been around someone who really loves and cares for you? This satisfies.

As we build relationships, we need to say, "Father, I will come to you on your conditions." As this relationship with God is established vertically, out of it we can establish many lasting, meaningful relationships horizontally.

DON'T BE TROUBLED OVER CIRCUMSTANCES

You do not have to be frustrated or anxious or troubled by circumstances that come your way. Since nothing can come into the life of a believer without God's permission, it comes with his grace to deal with it.

But how do we appropriate God's grace? One day at a time. "As thy days, so shall thy strength be" (Deut. 33:25, KJV).

Jesus said, "If anyone wishes to come after Me, let him deny himself, and take up His cross, and follow Me" (Matt. 16:24). We must do this daily. But there is a problem. Most of our lives are crucified between two thieves, yesterday and tomorrow. We never live today. But the time to live is now. It is today.

Jesus said, "Unless you repent, you will all likewise perish" (Luke 13:3). To repent means to change one's attitude toward God, toward sin, and toward others. God demands this. If our attitudes change, our lifestyles will also change.

My father was a wise, very quiet Texas rancher. His word was his bond. I never heard him utter a blasphemous word, and he was a total Christian.

Dad wore big, black boots with his khaki pants tucked into them. His black belt with the "W.O.T." initialed gold buckle was the one my mother gave him when they were married. With grey shirt, black, batwing tie, and Stetson hat, he rode the pasture.

I said, "Dad, a tie? It is hot!"

"Looks good," he said.

I would ask, "Who is looking? The cows?" This was my father. This was W. O. Thompson.

My father often told me to do things. If I did the task, but not well, he would say, "Son, you need to give more thought . . ." He did not chastise me for the way I did things. He was not as concerned about how I did something as he was about my attitude toward doing it.

If my attitude was not good, he would say, "I do not like your attitude. Change it." Friend, that meant change it. He would say, "You are in control of your attitude. You change it now."

"Yes, sir."

Now when God tells you or me to repent, he wants a change of attitude. He wants it now. We need to get into agreement with God in our attitudes and in our actions through obedience. We need to get right with God.

ARE YOU SURE GOD LOVES YOU?

Several years ago I was diagnosed with a disease that was expected to take my life within weeks. A student stood at the foot of my hospital bed and said, "Dr. Thompson, if this were to happen to me, I think I would be very bitter toward God. Look at all you have sought to do for him."

But I said, "Wait a minute, dear friend; you are not sure God loves you."

"Oh, yes, I am sure God loves me," he said.

"No," I said. "You are not sure God loves you because when you are sure God loves you, you realize that perfect love casts out all fear. Nothing can ever come into the life of a Christian without God's permission. And if God permits it, then he will give the grace and strength to deal with it."

Whatever our circumstances, if we seek God, he will begin to show us that we can rest in his love. Then anything that comes into our lives can be used for his glory.

"Father, as we reach out into our concentric circles, show us the barriers in our lives that need to be overcome. Help us be obedient to you and take comfort in your love."

FROM GOD TO SELF AND OTHERS

The beginning stage for making disciples is that you must get right with God, self, and others. When your vertical relationship with God is right, he will begin helping you get a proper perspective of who you are in Christ. He will help you get to know the real you. Out of this foundation of a right relationship with God and a strong and proper view of self, God can begin to flow through your life to others. Let's turn our attention to getting a right view of self. Then we will turn our attention to getting right with others.

PERSONALIZING CHAPTER 5

Using a journal or notebook, respond to the following questions or activities. Record details that will help you understand and apply the truths of this chapter to your own life.

1. Take time to pray and ask God about your relationship with him. Ask him to reveal the true nature of that relationship. Do you have a saving faith in his Son Jesus Christ? Are you in agreement with him in your daily walk? Are you living in obedience to him? Are you trusting him daily to give you victory over sin?

2. Based on what God reveals to you about your relationship, if you need to get right with him, do it now. Repent and turn away from any known sin. Choose afresh to make Christ Lord of your life daily.

3. Being right with God is not just a religious activity of keeping a list of dos and don'ts. God wants a love relationship with you. The best way to cultivate that relationship is by spending time with him. Take some extended time (up to an hour) just to talk with your heavenly Father. Find a quiet place at home or outside where you can talk to him. Ask him what he would like to do in your life. Share with him your cares, your joys, your questions, and your needs.

BUILDING UP THE BODY

Use the following questions and activities with your small group to help one another apply these truths to your lives and to build up the body of Christ.

1. Volunteers: Tell of an experience when you had to get right with God. What were the circumstances? How did God reveal your need to get right with him? How did you respond to him?

2. Tell of a time when you felt (and experienced) a close personal relationship with your heavenly Father. What are some ways you experience that closeness on a regular basis?

3. Suppose you were to meet a "Hollywood producer" (or anyone) who asked you, "What are God's conditions for me to come to him?" What would you say to him?

4. What have you done or experienced in the past week as a result of our study thus far? How is God working in your relationships?

5. Ask each small-group member: *How can we pray for you this week?* Then take time to pray for those specific needs or requests.

Chapter Six

CIRCLE 1:
GET RIGHT WITH SELF

Let's discuss self and what keeps the divine flow of God's love moving through it. If self is not right, no matter what methodology we use, we have problems. Self is your biggest problem and my biggest problem. In the natural economy of the self, we say, "I love *me,* and I want you to make *me* happy." Isn't that nice? As long as you meet my conditions, everything is going to be all right. The only problem with that is that it will not work!

GOD'S DESIGN FOR YOU

We are designed for fellowship with the King—God himself. Like the bird was made for the air and the fish was made for the sea, people were created for fellowship with God. Nothing is going to satisfy the deepest needs of our being until we have fellowship with him. This right relationship with him in turn will result in the right kind of fellowship with others on God's conditions.

THE UNREAL SELF

We first learn about relationships in the home. We can play games when we are at school and at work and so on. We can wear masks with people, but we are always changing our masks. With one person we are a certain way, with another person we are a certain way, and in business we are a certain way. We feel we have to be a certain way if we want to elicit a specific type of response from a client or an employer or employee. Consequently, we wear different masks, and after a while we forget which mask we have worn with what person. Suddenly we do a switch and people think, *Wow!*

Have you ever done that? Now do not sit there and look so pious. I know better. See, that is our problem. How can others develop a meaningful relationship with an unreal person? You must allow God to help you become the real person he intends for you to be.

LOVING YOURSELF

First of all, God wants you to feel good about you. He doesn't want you to try and cover up the real you. The Scriptures say, "YOU SHALL LOVE YOUR NEIGHBOR AS YOURSELF" (Matt. 19:19). You cannot love others without first loving yourself. You have to feel good about you.

God wants you to feel good about you. He wants you to love you. That sounds strange, doesn't it? What do you do when you love you? In Ephesians, Paul told husbands to love their wives as they love their own bodies (5:28). Do you stand in front of the mirror and say, "Oh, I just love me"? No! You do not get goose pimplish over looking at yourself in the mirror. If you do, you have a problem.

What you do when you love yourself is to meet your own needs. You feed yourself, cleanse yourself, brush yourself, shine yourself, paint yourself, clothe yourself, warm yourself, and cool yourself. Is there anything wrong with any of those things? Of course not. That is loving yourself. God wants us to take care of ourselves. Love is meeting needs.

As we mature, we take on a family, and God teaches us how to meet one another's needs. That is the reason God gave mothers and fathers babies. In the home, people learn how the Holy Father works so that they can meet the needs of little ones. As those little ones have their needs met, they know they are loved.

YOU AND YOUR INFERIORITY COMPLEX

As pastor consultant for the Cancer Research and Counseling Foundation, I once spoke at a medical convention. I was talking about stress and its effects when I commented: "According to an industrial psychologist, 95 percent of the people, by the time they are six years old, have inferiority complexes. They are not sure about themselves." One of my colleagues stopped me. He told me that I was wrong. That always makes a person feel good! He said, "It is not 95 percent. It is 100 percent! Every child by the time he is six years old has an inferiority complex." This may well be true.

As a child grows up, he says, "How do I feel about me?" A child may take a number of approaches. He may be aggressive, and adults conclude that he feels secure in himself. He knows who he is. He is all right. Often that is nothing more than his trying to get attention because he is not sure of himself. Then on the flip side is the child who becomes a wallflower and is afraid to say anything. He is shy. I am taking into consideration the various types of personalities. Now, we make so many mistakes in judging a Christian's life. We meet this gangbuster fellow who is a salesman and could sell snow cones to the Eskimos. We say, "Boy, if he were ever saved, he would really be great." Maybe he would, and maybe he would not.

Do not think that aggressiveness is necessarily spirituality. Some of the most passive people and passive types of personalities are very secure in themselves and are great channels of love. We do not see them, but oh, how God uses them.

Remember another thing. When you are converted, God does not change your personality. He changes your character. There is a vast difference. He wants you to be you. But he wants to be Christ in you. He wants to reach out through you and love through you.

All of us, you see, were born with the first Adam's nature. Its allegiance has three words, all personal pronouns: *me, my,* and *mine.* We carry this nature into business. Get all you can, can all you get, sit on the can, and do not share it with anybody else. It's just me, my, mine. That is the old Adamic nature.

WE NEED TO BE BALANCED

The self seeks balance. Our lives are much like a seesaw. The balance represents you. It represents me. The problems of life come, and pressure

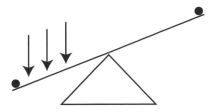

Pressures and problems push down on us.

pushes us down to make us think less of ourselves. We feel guilty, and guilt pushes the old Adamic nature farther down.

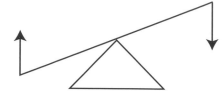

Old nature uses wrong ways to get back up.

That old Adamic nature wants to get back up, but that nature uses the wrong ways to get back up.

This cycle begins at an early age. All we want is to be balanced, but someone else gets on our little seesaw and begins to criticize us, to push us back down. Any kind of criticism causes an immediate reaction. If you hit me, I am going to do what? I am going to hit you back! You criticize me, and I am going to say that you are not so hot either. These reactions are natural, normal results of self-compensation—I am going to take care of me.

When someone tries to help us, we are sensitive and insecure. We think others are pushing us down, so we work to push ourselves back up again. I am not trying to be psychological. I am trying to be biblical. Then, when we begin to react toward other people, we begin to sense a feeling of control. If we have natural abilities, we use that control for our own selfish interests.

WHY DO WE INTIMIDATE OTHERS?

The aggressive person with a deep inferiority complex must dominate everybody else and run the show. He intimidates others in the church, in the family, or in business because that makes him feel better about himself.

Many little country churches get into a family hierarchical structure. They become the only place some people can have authority. But God never gets the glory, and these people hurt all their days, trying to suck the juices out of the situation just to run the show. Isn't that tragic?

Some things, such as guilt, push us down. There are two types of guilt: real guilt and self-imposed guilt. Real guilt is the guilt before God. I have sinned against the Lord; I have broken his laws; I have been self-centered. This is real guilt.

The other is self-imposed guilt. You can receive forgiveness for real guilt, but you cannot receive forgiveness for self-imposed guilt. Some of you have let God forgive you, but you have never forgiven yourself. Consequently, you are not sure that God has forgiven you. So you hurt.

With self-imposed guilt pressing us down, we make our plans but they come unglued. We put all of our eggs into one basket, but all of a sudden that basket comes apart. Then all we have are egg shells. We invest our lives in things, and in the end there is nothing. Why? Here is what I tell my young students.

SEEKING ACHIEVEMENT

One thing a person might use to pull himself back up after being pushed down is achievement. Achievement will pull me back up and help me feel balanced. If I am an achiever, people will not criticize me. They will praise me, and that praise will lift me up. So I must become an achiever.

Nothing is wrong with achievement. You were designed to be an achiever. You were designed for accomplishment. Why? To glorify God. Most of us want to achieve so that we can feel good about ourselves. I want to feel so good about me that I can raise myself up and look above my peers. Now I am a little higher, so I can look down on other people. Have you ever done that?

I really try to rattle the cage of my young preachers about this. I say, "You fellows go out into the association. You try to baptize more people, raise more money, build more buildings, and do all of these things. Because you have great native ability, you do them. You are so proud. You have done a good job. But you have done it for the wrong motivation. When you stand before God, such work is not going to be gold, silver, and precious stones; it is going to be hay, wood, and stubble."

Many of us serve God out of a guilty conscience. Our pastor tells us that we need to witness and we need to serve. We have guilty consciences. We have not served God, so we get busy in church and work so that we can get status and can feel good about ourselves. Have you ever seen that syndrome? What is the problem with all of this?

Some people go out into the business world. Some people go out in the academic world. Some people go out—! I have seen fellows work on doctor's degrees just so they could be called "doctor." The only reason they wanted a doctor's degree was for status, so that they could feel good about themselves. They were not working to gain skills to work more effectively in a place where God could put them.

I want you to read about an achiever in Ecclesiastes 2:1–10. What a pessimistic fellow! Listen to his conclusions regarding his achievements:

I said to myself, "Come now, I will test you with pleasure. So enjoy yourself." And behold, it too was futility. I said of laughter, "It is madness," and of pleasure, "What does it accomplish?" I explored with my mind how to stimulate my body with wine while my mind was guiding me wisely, and how to take hold of folly, until I could see what good there is for the sons of men to do under heaven the few years of their lives. I enlarged my works: I built houses for myself, I planted vineyards for myself; I made gardens and parks for myself, and I planted in them all kinds of fruit trees; I made ponds of water for myself from which to irrigate a forest of growing trees. I bought male and female slaves, and I had homeborn slaves. Also I possessed flocks and herds larger than all who preceded me in Jerusalem. Also, I collected for myself silver and gold, and the treasure of kings and provinces. I provided for myself male and female singers and the pleasures of men—many concubines. Then I became great and increased more than all who preceded me in Jerusalem. My wisdom also stood by me. And all that my eyes desired I did not refuse them. I did not withhold my heart from any pleasure, for my heart was pleased because of all my labor and this was my reward for all my labor.

This guy had "I" trouble. He had VISA, MasterCard, Carte Blanche. He had a blank check, no limit. You say, "Wouldn't that be great?" Not necessarily. Listen to more: "Thus I considered all my activities which my hands had done and the labor which I had exerted, and behold all was vanity and striving after wind and there was no profit under the sun" (Eccles. 2:11).

Well, should he never have done those things? No! But you see, he wanted them for the wrong reason: *I, me, my, mine.* Crunch! You say, "What does all of this have to do with evangelism?" Everything. Because you see, there is a flow of life in every life. The flow is either through you or to you. Jesus told us that out of our "innermost being shall flow rivers of living water" (John 7:38). But you see, the flow cannot flow through you when you are wanting it always to flow to you. We are not going to win the world around us when we are not sure about our own private world.

Topped-Out Achievers. Now the problem with achievement is that a person can climb the ladder. Most people never top out, and there are some relatively happy people who live all of their lives and are successful in that they have homes and cars and families. They raise a good family with moderate success, and they are not religious. We see the exterior of their lives.

Most people are so busy climbing that they do not know if they are happy or not. Sometimes a man is so busy making a business that he forgets his family obligations. As one old country preacher used to say, "Some fellows are so concerned about white-faced cows that they have completely forgotten about their white-faced boys." They are concerned about things rather than God. Why? Because they are not balanced.

Nothing is wrong with achievement. God wants us to achieve. He wants us to be the best business people we can be, the best teachers, or the best anything. That is fine.

But why? The achievement syndrome may top out, and many of the people do top out. Ernest Hemingway did. He was the top writer in the world, had married several times, and lived as he pleased. One writer said of him ten years before his death, "Here is the man who has broken all the laws and proved that sin does pay." But, three years before his death, he lost three-quarters of his mental ability and ended his life by blowing his brains out. A Marilyn Monroe, an Elvis Presley—you name them—they topped out from boredom. So after a person has done all there is to do and he tops out, where does he go? There is no place to go. He is still looking for achievement, but it is not there.

Bottomed-Out Underachievers. We have the two extremes, do we not? People top out, and people bottom out. At both extremes they say, "I do not want to live any more." These are the ones with suicidal tendencies.

This is where we find so many people in our affluent society. Due to failures, reversals, illness, laziness, or any number of other things, people hit bottom in utter failure and hopelessness.

CREATING AN ARTIFICIAL WORLD

Another thing a person might do to push himself back up is to create for himself an artificial world. He can do this in a number of ways. If he does not like his world, then he begins to daydream and fantasize about a world that pleases him. The psychologists used to call this neurosis.

All of us are a little neurotic. "All the world is peculiar except me and thee, and sometimes I think thou art a bit peculiar too!" So we begin to daydream.

It is all right to build air castles; just do not move into them. If you do, you begin to back off from reality and move into psychosis. You seek escape from the reality of the world around you. I have seen people retreat. They back off from the reality of life. They cannot take it.

Another way a person creates an artificial lifestyle is by saying, "I do not like the way I am; I do not feel good about me." He cannot face himself, so he begins to live a radically different lifestyle.

Alcohol becomes an escape mechanism for some people. They drink because they are exhausted from the pressures of the day. "I'll have a cool one; it will relax my nerves." Instead, alcohol becomes an escape mechanism. But escapees do not know how to get back to the real world.

Still another way to create an artificial world is through drugs. It is the same song as alcohol, but the second verse. Taking drugs is only a person running from the reality of saying, "I must be balanced."

THE SPIRITUAL ONES

Do not throw rocks at people who hurt like this. If you are hurting like this, I don't want to throw rocks at you either. I want to meet your needs. One problem in our world is that we have judged all these folk:

- the "mask" who hides the real person
- the intimidator with an inferiority complex
- the self-centered achiever
- the topped-out achiever
- the bottomed-out underachiever
- the neurotic daydreamer
- the psychotic who has escaped reality
- the person who has created an alternate lifestyle looking for meaning
- the alcoholic or drug addict who flees reality

Do not go to another man who is caught in sin with an attitude of "I am holy and look at me." If you do, all you are trying to accomplish is to give yourself undue praise. But I will show you a spiritual man. "Brethren, even if a man is caught in any trespass, you who are spiritual, restore such a one in a spirit of gentleness; each one looking to yourself, lest you too be tempted" (Gal. 6:1).

If you find a spiritual Christian, you will see someone who is reaching out to a man gently and saying, "Look, brother, I am just one beggar telling another beggar where we can both find bread." That is meeting needs. There is the holiness of God.

The essence of this whole thing is that God says, "You restore one; you reach out." Couldn't we all say, "Except by the grace of God, there go I"? Isn't that right? When a church is filled with people who act like that spiritual man, it begins to explode rather than implode. We begin to reach out. We begin to love. We begin to meet needs all around us.

Our teenagers get started on drugs, fall into sexual immorality, and do all sorts of unhealthy things because of that inferiority complex. Why? Because they want to be accepted. They want to feel good about themselves. If they do not know who they are, if they are not balanced, they are dependent upon the acceptance of their peer group. So they yield to the peer group. A guy who feels good about himself does not need to go along with the crowd.

Some kids say, "I do not want to be a holy Joe. I want to go through high school and have the kids like me without surrendering my Christian testimony, but how do I deal with that bunch?" The answer is very simple. Just say, "Look, you want me to smoke a joint with you? I want to thank you for wanting to include me in your group. That means so much to me, but let me tell you something. If I do that, I am going to hurt somebody I love very, very much. If you genuinely want me to be your friend and want to include me, you do not want me to hurt somebody I love very much, do you?"

Put the ball in their court without condemning them. I have had teenager after teenager come back and say, "Hey, that works." You do not isolate. You do not condemn them. You just reach out to them and say, "I have somebody I do not want to hurt." Doing this makes a difference.

ACHIEVING BALANCE

How do we achieve balance? This is an oversimplification, but here it is. When someone blames me, what do I do to push me up? If I know Jesus Christ, *I take this blame to the cross.* I can say, "Okay, Lord Jesus, thank you so much for loving me." If this person is right, you go to that person and say, "You are exactly right. I am a clod. I did say something wrong. Will you forgive me?" Then go to the cross. You are then clear and clean and balanced and do not have a running battle with anyone or ruptured relationships anywhere. Remember, if you are going to come to the balance that Jesus offers, you must come to the cross; die to self; die to

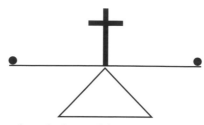

Life is balanced by Jesus Christ.

me, my, and *mine;* and let him be Lord. Jesus Christ brings balance to your life.

Then, even if someone does blame us and if we are not guilty, we take that to the cross too. We do not let bitterness build up.

You say, "But he criticizes me all the time." Well, so what? If you know who you are in Christ, who cares? If your heavenly Father—the Creator of the universe—loves you, cares for you, and accepts you, that is enough! The person who is balanced is not devastated by criticism. He knows who he is in his relationship with God. He can rest in his relationship with Jesus Christ.

You need to know that when you start living a holy life and God begins to love through you, some people are going to be upset. Because your lifestyle is going to rise higher than their lifestyles, they are going to feel bad about their lifestyles. Your lifestyle condemns theirs. Their inferiority complex gets irritated, and they try to put you down to start feeling better about themselves. They will start throwing rocks. You could get upset and say, "What is this?" But you just love them. You don't fight back. You don't say, "Yes, I am pretty holy, aren't I?" As Charles Spurgeon said, "We always thought this brother was humble until one day he told us he was."

Why do you achieve? Why do you want to make straight A's in school? God made you to be the best you can be, so do not feel guilty. Do not compare yourself with anyone else. You are like a snowflake. You are like a fingerprint. You are you. You are not to compare yourself with anyone else. You are one of a kind. God made you to be you.

Some preachers are always comparing themselves with other preachers. But God did not make us alike. God did not make me like Billy Graham. He made me Oscar Thompson. I cannot help it. I do not want to help it. I am who I am. I must be me. If I am not me in God's economy, then I am wrong in my attitude. I must accept the way I am. When Jesus fills me, I can accept me. I can be balanced.

I tell my preachers, "Do not go out there and say I wish I were like . . ." No, you are blaming God if you do not like the way God made you. God has a ministry and a plan for you. I do not care how great that other fellow's ministry is. You be faithful in the things you can do. You are not to judge yourself by your peer group. Do not be condemned by anybody else's standards. You are you.

Do not worry about that achievement level either. You achieve for the glory of God. As you achieve, lay your successes at his feet. Isn't that sweet? Do all that you do to the glory of God.

Now, if we can achieve that balance, we will achieve it at the cross. That is why I glory in the cross. That is why Jesus died for me. That is where I can find forgiveness of sin. That is where I do not have to blame anyone else. That is where God's goodness and love flow to me. That is where I find achievement. I do not have to be frustrated, comparing myself with a thousand other people. I am who I am.

"Thank you, Father. Now take me and flow through me beyond myself in Circle 1 to my concentric circles."

PERSONALIZING CHAPTER 6

Using a journal or notebook, respond to the following questions or activities. Record details that will help you understand and apply the truths of this chapter to your own life.

1. When have you ever acted in one of the following ways because you were hurting and feeling bad about yourself? What was the hurt or emptiness like?
   - the "mask" who hides the real person
   - the intimidator with an inferiority complex
   - the self-centered achiever
   - the topped-out achiever
   - the bottomed-out underachiever
   - the neurotic daydreamer
   - the psychotic who has escaped reality
   - the person who has created an alternate lifestyle looking for meaning
   - the alcoholic or drug addict who flees reality
2. If you are still living in one of these ways, decide to turn away from that false self and turn to the Lord. Ask him to heal the brokenness

or fill the emptiness. Ask him to help you experience his love, forgiveness, and acceptance in such a way that your inferiority complex disappears. Ask him to help you accept the "you" he created you to be. Ask him to bring balance into your life.

3. Perhaps God has already done this healing work in you. Do you know people who are living and acting like those listed in #1 above? Add them to your survey of concentric circles. Begin to pray that God would love them through you. Watch for ways you can encourage them, bless them, and lift them up through your words and actions.

4. Practice going to the cross. Let the following actions become an alarm system that alerts you to go to the cross for help in responding in the right way. Write notes in your journal or notebook of actions you will take if any of these experiences are common in your life:

   • When someone blames, accuses, or corrects you for something for which you are guilty, go to the cross. Agree with the person and with God about your sin and ask for forgiveness. Decide, with God's help, to not commit that sin again. Receive God's forgiveness and don't revisit that issue again.

   • When someone blames, accuses, or corrects you for something you are not guilty of, go to the cross. Before God, make sure you are not guilty. Let God remind you of his love and acceptance. Thank God for the privilege of suffering like Jesus when he was falsely accused. Don't get bitter. Don't try to get even. Lay your case before the Lord and let him lift you up.

   • When you are so wounded or hurt by reality that you want to run away or escape, go to the cross. Get alone with God and tell him all about your problems. Cast your cares and anxieties on him. Tell him you can't make it without his help. Ask him for strength to endure. Ask him to use the experience to make you more like Jesus by refining your life, by breaking away self and pride.

   • When your inferiority complex attacks and you feel worthless, unloved, inadequate, or inferior, go to the cross. Let God remind you that he loved you so much that Jesus went to the cross for you. Let God remind you that he chose you and adopted you into his family. Let him remind you that you are his masterpiece of creation and that he doesn't make "junk." Take your thoughts captive and make them obedient to Christ (speak God's truth about yourself instead of the lies of the world) (see 2 Cor. 10:3–5).

- When you realize you are being driven to achieve, go to the cross. Ask the Lord to help you evaluate your motives. Ask him to prune from your life every desire to achieve that doesn't come from him. Decide to do only those things that he desires, and do them for his glory alone.
- When you despise who you are and you envy someone else, go to the cross. Ask the Lord to remind you of the real you he created you to be. Ask him if there are corrections he wants to make in the unreal you that will help you become more the person he created you to be. Ask him if this other person has godlike qualities that God wants to develop in you. Pray for the other person that God will continue to bless and use him or her for his own glory.

BUILDING UP THE BODY

Use the following questions and activities with your small group to help one another apply these truths to your lives and to build up the body of Christ.

1. Read James 5:16—"Therefore, confess your sins to one another, and pray for one another, so that you may be healed. The effective prayer of a righteous man can accomplish much." Ask: Based on your response to #1 under Personalizing Chapter 6, what are some ways you are hurting or feeling bad about yourself? How have those feelings caused you to act in ways you know are displeasing to the Lord? As individuals respond, take time to surround them with prayer. You might even lay hands on their shoulders as you pray to let them know of your concern and support. Allow more than one person to pray for each person who shares. Pray for each individual until you come to a confident assurance that God will accomplish the spiritual healing needed.
2. Discuss the ways in which God is leading you to "go to the cross." When do you believe God may use the alarm system described above to invite you to come to the cross for help?
3. What are some ways God can work through Christians to encourage and build one another up? Do you need to take time to practice these right now with your group? If so, do it!
4. What have you done or experienced in the past week as a result of our study thus far? How is God working in your relationships?
5. Ask each small-group member: *How can we pray for you this week?* Then take time to pray for these specific needs or requests.

Chapter Seven

*B*EARING *S*PIRITUAL *F*RUIT

THE REAL PURPOSE IN LIFE

When we look at life—and the last few years I have had many opportunities to look at the length as well as the brevity of life with many people—I think we need to pinpoint our priorities. Too much of our lives, too much of our ministries, are frittered away on nonessentials. If we are to do what God calls us to do in the time that he has given us to do it, we must know our priorities. We must zero in on them and accomplish them. Jesus sets the priority.

We all need checklists to accomplish things correctly. I remember what my flight instructor said to me when I was first learning to fly: "This is your checklist. You are a young pilot, but if you want to live to be an old pilot, you will always use your checklist."

For the Christian, I feel John 15:1–12 is a checklist. I have found that when I feel out of touch, out of focus, out of sorts, I should go back to my checklist. Jesus said:

> I AM the true vine, and My Father is the vinedresser. Every branch in Me that does not bear fruit, He takes away; and every branch that bears fruit, He prunes it, that it may bear more fruit. You are already clean because of the word which I have spoken to you. Abide in Me, and I in you. As the branch cannot bear fruit of itself, unless it abides in the vine, so neither can you, unless you abide in Me. I am the vine, you are the branches; he who abides in Me, and I in him, he bears much fruit; for apart from Me you can do nothing. If anyone does not abide in Me, he is thrown away as a branch, and dries up; and they gather them, and cast them into the fire, and they are burned. If you abide in Me, and My words abide in you, ask

whatever you wish, and it shall be done for you. By this is My Father glorified, that you bear much fruit, and so prove to be My disciples. Just as the Father has loved Me, I have also loved you; abide in My love. If you keep My commandments, you will abide in My love; just as I have kept My Father's commandments, and abide in His love. These things I have spoken to you, that My joy may be in you, and that your joy may be made full. This is My commandment, that you love one another, just as I have loved you.

The purpose for your occupying space and taking up oxygen, your reason for existence, is to bear fruit. If you are not bearing fruit, there is no reason for your existence.

The Word says that if you want to glorify the Father, you will bear fruit. If you want to demonstrate that you are his disciple, you will bear fruit. If you want to be a blessing to the world, you will bear fruit.

This is such an important parable for every Christian to understand. I believe that Jesus was not talking about being saved or lost in John 15. He was talking about a Christian bearing fruit. Jesus used the image of fruit bearing because the people knew what he was talking about. He was reaching into their world so that he could communicate with them. In our present economy and way of life, we do not understand much about vines and grapes. We have to translate both the idea of the fruit and the idea that Jesus is conveying into language we can understand.

WHAT IS SPIRITUAL FRUIT?
- "Is it service for the Lord?" No.
- "Is it attending services or praying?" No.
- "Is it souls we have won?" No.
- "Is it buildings, baptisms, or budgets?" No.

These things overflow from fruit, but they are not what we are talking about when we say "bearing fruit."

Fruit always comes from the nature of the seed. The nature of the seed will also be the nature of the fruit. If you plant a peach pit, you will get a peach tree. If you plant a plum seed, you will get a plum tree. And I suppose that if there were a spaghetti seed and you planted it, you would get a spaghetti plant.

Fruit comes from the nature of the seed, and the seed is the Word of God. It is the person of God and his written Word. "In the beginning was the Word, and the Word was with God, and the Word was God. . . . All things came into being by Him, and apart from Him nothing came into being that has come into being" (John 1:1, 3).

The Word of God tells us that God wants to produce his character in our lives. So to bear fruit means that we allow the character of God to be produced in our lives. In Galatians 5:22–23, Paul taught that the fruit of the Spirit is:

- Love—the relationship
- Joy—the result of the relationship
- Peace—the result of the correct relationship
- Patience (long-suffering)—the maintenance of the relationship
- Kindness—the attitude of the relationship
- Goodness—the outgoing blessing of the relationship
- Faithfulness—the means of the relationship
- Gentleness (meekness)—the submitted will in the relationship
- Self-Control—the control of the relationship

So the nature of the seed, the nature of the Word, the nature of God will be reproduced in the life of the believer. If that does not happen, there is a major problem in the life of the believer.

The fruit is the very character of God. Jesus came to earth and he lived his life.

- What he saw his Father do is what he did: "'Truly, truly, I say to you, the Son can do nothing of Himself, unless it is something He sees the Father doing; for whatever the Father does, these things the Son also does in like manner'" (John 5:19).
- What he heard his Father say is what he said: "'Do you not believe that I am in the Father, and the Father is in Me? The words that I say to you I do not speak on My own initiative, but the Father abiding in Me does His works. Believe me that I am in the Father, and the Father in Me; otherwise believe on account of the works themselves'" (John 14:10–11).

Jesus was in total submission to and in union with the Father. As a result of that submission, the Father manifested his character in Jesus. Jesus came to earth not only to die for us but also to manifest the character of the Father so that people can see what God is like.

THE PARABLE OF THE PURPLE MARTINS

I have a beautiful martin house on a little hill in my backyard. It is for purple martins, birds who eat their weight in mosquitoes and other pesky insects each day. It sits on a telescoping pole. Several months ago, when I was out of town, one of the nuts on the pole slipped; the martin house dropped down. When I got back home, I found it about four feet off the ground.

The martins did not seem bothered by the slippage; but I was afraid the cats would get to them, so I went out to raise it. Of course, I was staring the birds right in the face. They scattered like a covey of quail and really fussed at me. I ran the pole all the way up and secured it. But one old bird in that group decided I had done something terribly wrong.

Now every time I walk into the backyard, she flies to about sixty feet and dives at me, coming within twelve inches of my head. Then just as she passes my head, she goes "chirrup!" She does not bother my daughter Damaris. She does not bother our puppies, Burfaldine or Neigette. She does not bother Carolyn, and she does not bother our guests. Just me!

I was standing in the backyard several days later when I said to the bird, "You dummy, don't you know I was lifting your house back up so a cat, skunk, or whatever could not bother your babies?" But she, like some fighter plane coming out of a cloud, just dived down and buzzed right over my head. I said, "I wish I could communicate with you, but I cannot. I do not know bird language." I tried it. I went "chirrup," but she just kept coming back.

Do you get the point? God said, "I want to communicate with people." So, Jesus Christ entered history. In John 1:14 we read that Jesus is the Word. God sent Jesus to build a bridge to people, to communicate with them, to develop a relationship with them. Jesus is the One who reveals the character of the Father. Isn't that beautiful? Jesus built the bridge between God and people so that we can have a relationship with God.

THE NATURE OF JESUS

Bearing fruit is the nature of Jesus being revealed in your life. I once heard someone ask a black man, "What is a Christian?"

He smiled and replied, "Just Jesus running around in a black body." Or a white one, or a red one, or a yellow one, or whatever else.

Bearing fruit is Jesus Christ manifesting his character in our lives, Jesus' lifestyle in us. Jesus wants his lifestyle to be manifested in your life.

Remember, Paul said that God has given to us two things: the Word of reconciliation and the ministry of reconciliation (see 2 Cor. 5:18–19). Our lives are to be linked with God since God linked us with himself by his grace and by the cross. He gives us the ability to reach out and build bridges to a lost world. That is what life is all about. That is bearing fruit.

When your life is bearing his fruit, you are bearing his life. You do not produce the fruit; he does. You bear it.

Jesus said, "I am the vine, you are the branches" (John 15:5). In other words, you are a glorified grape rack. All you can do is bear the fruit. You cannot produce it. The vine, which is Jesus, produces it. Have you ever seen a tree saying, "Oh, I just have to produce some fruit"? No. It just does what it is designed to do.

RESULTS OF BEARING SPIRITUAL FRUIT

Three passages in John 15 tell about the results of bearing fruit. Let's give them some directions: Upward, inward, and outward.

UPWARD REACH—ANSWERED PRAYER

The first result of bearing spiritual fruit is the upward reach that results in answered prayer. Jesus said, "If you abide in Me, and My words abide in you, ask whatever you wish, and it shall be done for you" (John 15:7). A person who has fellowship and a close walk with the Lord Jesus Christ is going to live in a spirit and lifestyle of answered prayer. When he prays, things happen. One of the greatest marks of a Christian's life is that he has answered prayer.

Is God answering prayer in your life? Well, he cannot answer prayer unless you are praying. James reminds us, "You do not have because you do not ask" (James 4:2b). You will not bear much fruit if you are not spending time as an intercessor. I believe that the greatest battle in evangelism and in living for Jesus is prayer.

In fellowship with Jesus, knowing that I am dependent on the Father for everything, I come to him, spend time with him, and talk to him. Then his Holy Spirit reveals things in and through my life. It is of divine necessity that the believer be a great talker with God. Are you a person of prayer? Is prayer a major part of your strategy for bearing the spiritual fruit of Christ's life in yours? If not, you need to turn to the Lord and begin to pray until you experience the "it shall be done for you" of answered prayer.

INWARD JOY

The second result of bearing spiritual fruit is inward joy. In John 15:11 we read, "These things I have spoken to you, that My joy may be in you, and that your joy may be made full."

If you study the Beatitudes (Matt. 5:3–12), you will notice that Jesus uses the word *blessed* for each one:

Blessed are the poor in spirit, for theirs is the kingdom of heaven.

Blessed are those who mourn, for they shall be comforted.

Blessed are the gentle, for they shall inherit the earth.

Blessed are those who hunger and thirst for righteousness, for they shall be satisfied.

Blessed are the merciful, for they shall receive mercy.

Blessed are the pure in heart, for they shall see God.

Blessed are the peacemakers, for they shall be called sons of God.

Blessed are those who have been persecuted for the sake of righteousness, for theirs is the kingdom of heaven.

Blessed are you when men cast insults at you, and persecute you, and say all kinds of evil against you falsely, on account of Me.

Rejoice, and be glad, for your reward in heaven is great, for so they persecuted the prophets who were before you.

The word *blessed* is the Greek word *makarios*. This word was used for the Isle of Cyprus and meant that if a person lived in Cyprus, he had everything he could possibly need within the confines of that island. It was a blessed state. The people who lived there had a sense of satisfaction, a sense of fulfillment, and a sense of joy in that blessedness.

Dear friend, if you are walking in Jesus Christ and have found him sufficient, your life is filled with a sense of blessedness. That is inward joy.

I am not talking about joy in outward circumstances. Your outward circumstances may be terrible. Do not depend on happenings to make you happy. If things happen happy, you are happy. If they do not happen happy, you are not happy. No! If you live like this, your life will never be tranquil. You will never experience the joy God desires for you.

No matter what the outward circumstances are, joy is an inward relationship with God that gives peace and joy. Do you have inward joy? If you are bearing spiritual fruit, you will have inward joy.

Joy comes from a relationship with a person—from fellowship with the Lord. Remember that the most important word in the English language apart from proper nouns is *relationship*. A relationship with Jesus

Christ brings joy. That relationship with him will determine your relationships with others.

OUTWARD *AGAPE* LOVE

The third result of bearing spiritual fruit is outward *agape* love. Love is meeting needs. This kind of love comes from God's resources, not ours. We are going to bear this fruit of love, but we cannot produce it. Only he can produce this kind of love. We are only the channel of his love. God has never told us he loved us without meeting our needs.

- "God so *loved* the world, that He *gave* . . ." (John 3:16, author's italics).
- "God demonstrates His own love toward us, in that while we were yet sinners, *Christ died for us*" (Rom. 5:8, author's italics).
- "We know [the] *love* [of God] by this, that *He laid down His life for us*" (1 John 3:16, author's italics).
- "But God, being rich in mercy, because of His great love with which He loved us, even when we were dead in our transgressions, *made us alive*" (Eph. 2:4–5, author's italics).

Every time you find God loving us, he is meeting our needs. Loving people is meeting needs. Love may not be a feeling. Although *philia* [brotherly] love is tied to feelings, *agape* love does not depend on feelings. It is a commitment of the will saying, "I am going to meet those needs out of the resources of God." The feeling may follow, but it may not. The real essence of the love that Jesus spoke about—the love that will flow through us—is best illustrated in Jesus' words about how God loves.

In Matthew 5:45 Jesus talked about God's love for two farmers—one righteous and the other unrighteous. "He causes His sun to rise on the evil and the good, and sends rain on the righteous and the unrighteous." God loved them both and treated them both alike. There are no favorites with God.

You may say, "I am going to love the lost. I am going to love that person out there." No, dear friend, unless you are loving everybody in your circles, loving without discrimination, your love may not be flowing from the Holy Spirit. It may be an I-love-me-and-I-want-you-to-make-me-happy kind of love. Love that is conditional like that is not God's kind of love.

If I do not love (meet the needs) my daughter and my wife and those in my inner circles, then I am not loving as I should. Love for Jesus means I love everybody in sight. I love those for whom God has given me responsibility. It is my responsibility to meet the needs of Carolyn, whatever those needs are. It is my job to meet the needs of Damaris. I show God's love by meeting their needs.

As God brings people into my life, whoever they are, he brings them there for a purpose. God then says, "Now, Oscar, you meet their needs, not out of your resources, but out of mine. Let me love them through you." I become a channel for meeting needs. This is what Jesus was saying. If we are bearing spiritual fruit, we will be loving without discrimination. Our love will be unconditional like God's. We will be watching for opportunities to show God's love to every person in our concentric circles.

Do you know what? If we could get our churches to see that we are to love without discrimination and that we are to give the Holy Spirit liberty to love everybody in sight through us, then we would have revival on our hands! The world would turn aside to see the "burning bush."

PERSONALIZING CHAPTER 7

Using a journal or notebook, respond to the following questions or activities. Record details that will help you understand and apply the truths of this chapter to your own life.

1. Let God be your vinedresser (John 15:2), and examine your life and your spiritual fruit. Ask him to help you see what he sees.
   - Are you experiencing answers to your prayers? Are you praying?
   - Are you experiencing inward joy that is reflected to those who see your life, even when circumstances are bad?
   - Are you allowing God to love others through your life unconditionally?
2. The vinedresser also prunes (or cuts away) parts of the branches so they will be more fruitful. Ask God if there are activities in your life that he wants to cut away so you will be more fruitful. Are there activities that consume time in unproductive ways? Are you participating in nonessential activities that God wants to get rid of? Are you doing some good things that keep you too busy to do the things you sense God is calling you to do? As God reveals the things he wants to prune, choose to let go of those activities so you can be more fruitful.
3. Ask God to help you measure your spiritual fruit by the list Paul gave us in Galatians 5:22–23.
   - Love—the relationship
   - Joy—the result of the relationship

- Peace—the result of the correct relationship
- Patience (long-suffering)—the maintenance of the relationship
- Kindness—the attitude of the relationship
- Goodness—the outgoing blessing of the relationship
- Faithfulness—the means of the relationship
- Gentleness (meekness)—the submitted will in the relationship
- Self-Control—the control of the relationship

4. Ask God to teach you to abide in him so that he will abide in you. Ask him to reveal the nature and character of Jesus through your life for his glory.

BUILDING UP THE BODY

Use the following questions and activities with your small group to help one another apply these truths to your lives and to build up the body of Christ.

1. Volunteers: What has God revealed to you in this chapter about your own fruitfulness or lack of fruitfulness? What adjustments do you sense he is calling you to make so that you will be more fruitful?
2. Use the questions and activities in Personalizing Chapter 7 to examine (with God's help) the spiritual fruitfulness of your church. Looking at your church as a whole:
   - Would it be known for answered prayer, joy, and unconditional love?
   - Would it be known for love, joy, peace, patience, kindness, goodness, faithfulness, gentleness, and self-control?
   - Are there activities, attitudes, or programs that God would like to prune from your church to help you be more fruitful?
3. Based on your discussion and response to #2, spend some time as a group praying for your church and its fruitfulness. Pray for one another that you will each contribute to the fruitfulness of your church.
4. What have you done or experienced in the past week as a result of our study thus far? How is God working in your relationships?
5. Ask each small-group member: *How can we pray for you this week?* Then take time to pray for these specific needs or requests.

Chapter Eight

*H*INDRANCES TO *B*EARING *S*PIRITUAL *F*RUIT

All this discussion of bearing fruit may raise a question in your mind: Why am I not bearing fruit? Jesus revealed three hindrances to bearing fruit:

> Behold, the sower went out to sow; and as he sowed, some seeds fell beside the road, and the birds came and ate them up. And others fell upon the rocky places, where they did not have much soil; and immediately they sprang up, because they had no depth of soil. But when the sun had risen, they were scorched; and because they had no root, they withered away. And others fell among the thorns, and the thorns came up and choked them out. And others fell on the good soil, and yielded a crop, some a hundredfold, some sixty, and some thirty (Matt. 13:3–8).

In six short verses, Jesus presented the parable involving the stolen, the shallow, the choked, and the good seed.

THE STOLEN SEED: FAILING TO LET GOD'S WORD GERMINATE

Jesus said: "Hear then the parable of the sower. When anyone hears the word of the kingdom, and does not understand it, the evil one comes and snatches away what has been sown in his heart. This is the one on whom seed was sown beside the road" (Matt. 13:18–19).

Jesus said the sower went forth to sow. What happened? The sower sowed the seed, and the "evil one" came and stole the seed.

I want to ask you what your preacher preached last Sunday. What was taught in your Sunday school class? Listen very closely. The key in fruit bearing is the germination of the seed. It makes no difference how much seed is sown; if the seed does not germinate, it does not bear fruit.

Satan is not concerned with how many people gather in a service if all they do is sit and listen and leave. Satan does not care how much seed is sown as long as he can steal it away.

An encounter with the living God and with his Word needs to take place. The seed of the Word of God needs to be dropped into people's hearts and then germinated by faith. Then the Holy Spirit takes it and produces new life. The tragedy is that many people go to the services, fill the Sunday school classes, are counted in attendance, but then slip away. Their lives are no different. They bear no fruit. They do not touch the lost world, and they are not reconciling the world to Christ.

At this point we must assume two things. The parable of the sower assumes that the seed has been sown. It is a big assumption for our day, is it not? Many times no seed is sown. Those of you who are preachers and teachers, do not tell people what you think. Instead, tell them what the Word of God says. Open the Scriptures and make God's Word come alive for your people. If no seed is sown, there will be no germination.

I receive letters and telephone calls from people all over the country who say, "We need a preacher who will preach the Word." Now this means that we need men who are able to take the Scriptures and, in the power of the Holy Spirit, present them in such a way that they become alive, where people can understand and say, "I received a word from the Lord."

It is also the responsibility of the Sunday school teachers to make sure the Word of God has been shared in their classes. We must teach the Word of God. This mighty burden is on the pastor, on every Sunday school teacher, and on each proclaimer of the Word. Whatever your status, God holds you responsible for making sure that the people in your concentric circles know what God's Word says.

In Matthew 13:19 we have read that sowing the Word of God is not enough. There is a supernatural power afoot to snatch the Word of God away from us. Satan does not mind how much you have heard the Word, just as long as that Word does not fall into your heart and germinate and bring forth fruit.

Distraction from the Word of God is one of the greatest problems we have in the world today. If a pastor would be so bold as to stand at the back door and ask, "What did I preach this morning?" how many would remember?

A second problem is: though you may preach a masterful message, pastor, if the people in your congregation do not realize that the Word of God is to be meditated upon, it will not bear fruit. Meditation is taking the Word of God and covering it by faith so that it germinates like a seed, springs forth, and bears fruit.

Tragically, the Word is often stolen away. Do people carry the Word of God with them from their Sunday school classes or from the preaching services? Is the Word of God planted firmly so that God can encounter the human personality and the human soul? Whenever we try to remember a Scripture passage, a supernatural power will be afoot to steal it away.

Following Sunday services, the world will provide all kinds of distractions that can be used by Satan to snatch away the Word that has been sown. The distraction may be a football game, a movie, or a dinner with relatives. If people are not taught and encouraged to meditate on the Word they hear, they are likely to let it be stolen away before it has time to germinate.

THE SHALLOW SEED:
FAILING TO DEPEND ON GOD DURING TIMES OF TESTING

Let's look at Matthew 13:20–21. "The one on whom seed was sown on the rocky places, this is the man who hears the word, and immediately receives it with joy; yet he has no *firm* root in himself, but is *only* temporary, and when affliction or persecution arises because of the word, immediately he falls away."

Have you ever been in a service and heard a sermon that you felt the Lord sent just for you? It met your particular need—encouragement, correction, insight, or whatever. You were convicted and the Word germinated. It took hold.

Let me give you a spiritual principle: The moment the Word germinates and takes hold, the processes of nature take hold to see if the seed is going to bear fruit.

Let me explain. The sun comes out. Now isn't that what Jesus said in Matthew 13:6? The sun comes out and will test that seed. Is the sun there to destroy the seed? No. The sun is there to help that seed produce luxurious fruit. But the same sun that produces luxurious fruit in one seed scorches another plant, and it withers. In other words, the purpose of the testing is not to destroy the fruit, but to produce it.

Have you ever seen this happen? A set of circumstances moves into one believer's life and he remains or abides in Christ, soaks up the strength of the vine, takes the life of the vine, and produces the character of Christ.

Another person, under the same set of circumstances, does not abide in the vine as he should. He knows the principles, but instead of bearing fruit, he becomes bitter and hard and angry with God. He says, "Why has this happened to me? Why has this come?" His fruit withers and dies.

Has that ever happened to you? You see, God always takes his children and places them in circumstances that have potential for bearing fruit. How we react by faith determines the fruit. For example, you hear a sermon on "Love your neighbor." You really should love your neighbor, shouldn't you? The Scripture says that you are to love your neighbor. So you say, "I am going to love my neighbor."

You talk on the way home about how you are going to love your neighbors. You think about ways to give them attention. You are so happy. You get home, and guess who is standing in your driveway? One of your neighbors. He indignantly says, "Your dog just dug up all my daffodils!" The testing "sun" is out. Are you going to wither or bear fruit? Here is your opportunity. You see, any old Pharisee can love folk who love him. It does not take any of God's grace to love those who love you. But it takes God's supernatural grace to love those who do not love you.

The point is: after you receive a fresh, new insight into the Word of God, the Lord will allow that truth to be tested in your life. He will show you that he is adequate for any circumstance, just as his Word says he is. He wants you to bear fruit.

Every circumstance that comes into your life is an opportunity for God to demonstrate his power in your life. The heat comes—the heat of circumstances, the heat of persecution, the heat of wrong feelings. These crises come into your life. All of the circumstances swirl about you, and you think, *Lord, what happened?* Nothing. God is just trying to produce fruit in your life.

How many times have you wilted? How many times has God put you in a circumstance? You got an insight from his Word. You received it with joy. Then the test came, and you blew it.

If, as you begin to pray through your concentric circles, "all hell breaks loose," do not be alarmed. If, when you share with someone and the person chews you up one side and down the other, remember that God just wants to demonstrate his love and gentleness through you by your turning the other cheek (Matt. 5:39). Most people have never understood that passage. God wants to demonstrate his character in your life.

THE CHOKED SEED:
ALLOWING WORRY TO CONSUME OUR ENERGIES

"The one on whom seed was sown among the thorns, this is the man who hears the word, and the worry of the world, and the deceitfulness of riches choke the word, and it becomes unfruitful" (Matt. 13:22).

Does this seed germinate? Yes. Was it growing into a fine plant? Yes. But all of a sudden, other things choked it out. Did it bear fruit? No. Something choked it. What chokes us?

The number one problem we have is worry, little anxieties. You cannot praise God and worry at the same time. The word translated "worry" in verse 22 is *merimna*. This is a Greek word that runs through the Scriptures. It is used in Matthew 6:31, "Do not be anxious"; in 1 Peter 5:7, "Casting all your anxiety upon Him"; and in Philippians 4:6, "Be anxious for nothing."

In these verses, *merimna* means not to let anxiety eat at you. You are not to let it grasp you. If you leave a garden hoe out in the morning dew for several days, you will find that it has begun to rust. This is oxidation, and it has eaten into the hoe. This is the meaning of *merimna*. God is telling us not to let the corrosive cares of this world eat on us.

Are you anxious about business, about a child, about your marriage, or about many things? Then weeds are choking the seed, and you will not bear fruit.

One lady came to me and asked, "But Brother Oscar, why pray when I can worry?" Listen, friend, God gives us grace for one day at a time. Do not let the worries of tomorrow choke out the peace and joy of today. Worry will choke out the fruit. Remember that Jesus is our inheritance and that he will never allow anything to enter into our lives that he will not supply the grace and strength for us to bear it.

I remember going to a new church in my younger days as a pastor and having a deacon try to intimidate me. He said, "Unless you fire that educational director . . . ." But I do not fire educational directors, and I do not hire them. They come from the Lord.

This deacon said, "Unless you fire him, several families will leave the church."

I sort of grinned and put my arm around him and asked, "What are you trying to tell me?"

He answered, "Well, we will lose their tithes, and that might hurt your salary." Hear that old squeeze? I had been serving in this church only three weeks.

So I just hugged him real tight and said, "Let me tell you a secret."

"What is it?" he asked.

"I am independently wealthy," I whispered.

"You are?" he said.

I explained, "You see, my Father owns the cattle on a thousand hills. He sets my salary."

That man became my dearest friend. We did not lose one person, and I surely did not fire that good man who was trying to carry on a ministry that the church was too hardhearted to recognize.

BEARING MUCH SPIRITUAL FRUIT

"The one on whom seed was sown on the good soil, this is the man who hears the word and understands it; who indeed bears fruit, and brings forth, some a hundredfold, some sixty, and some thirty" (Matt. 13:23).

This person bears much fruit. What is the result of being filled with the Spirit? As was listed earlier, Christ's character is the fruit of the Spirit as seen in Galatians 5:22–23—love, joy, peace, patience (long-suffering), kindness, goodness, faithfulness, gentleness (meekness), and self-control.

If you are bearing fruit, remember these three directions: upward, inward, and outward. Remember also that God will never let anything come into your life except by his permission. If it comes with his permission, it comes with his grace and strength. But he gives that grace for one day at a time. What is your purpose for occupying space and taking up oxygen? What is your purpose for living? To bear spiritual fruit. If you do not bear fruit, then someday when you stand before him, your hands will be empty.

PERSONALIZING CHAPTER 8

Using a journal or notebook, respond to the following questions or activities. Record details that will help you understand and apply the truths of this chapter to your own life.

1. When God's Word and will are made known to you, what is the most common reason for your own failure to bear spiritual fruit?
   - I fail to meditate on God's Word and let it germinate in my mind, heart, and actions.
   - I depend on myself rather than on God when trials, testing, and persecution come. I don't have the strength to stand up under the load, so I wilt. I quit.

- I get caught up worrying about the cares, concerns, and needs of life. I spend all my energy on other things and I'm so worn out that I don't have time to attend to the things God has revealed.

2. Think about the times God has spoken through his Word to you and spiritual fruit came forth in your life. What was different in those times about your focus on God, your dependence on God, your obedience and devotion to God, your time with God?

3. Suppose God is a soil specialist and He is testing the soil of your life to see what "fertilizer" you need to be more fruitful. Ask God to reveal what you need to do differently so that his Word will be most fruitful in your life and ministry. Write notes in your journal or notebook on the things you sense he would have you do differently. By the way, are there any "weeds" he wants to remove from your life to prevent them from choking out his Word?

4. Before you allow Satan to steal God's Word from this chapter (and the last few chapters) from you, get alone with God and meditate on what he has been saying to you. Review your journal or notebook. Review your responses to personalizing the chapters. Begin taking the actions God is leading you to take so the seed will grow strong.

BUILDING UP THE BODY

Use the following questions and activities with your small group to help one another apply these truths to your lives and to build up the body of Christ.

1. Describe experiences where each of the three hindrances to spiritual fruit bearing have robbed you of spiritual fruit. What could have been done differently in each case to cooperate with God in bearing fruit?

2. Invite volunteers to explain their responses to activities 2 and 3 in Personalizing Chapter 8.

3. How has time alone with your heavenly Father meditating on his Word made a specific difference in your spiritual fruitfulness? Describe one such experience.

4. What have you done or experienced in the past week as a result of our study thus far? How is God working in your relationships?

5. Ask each small-group member: *How can we pray for you this week?* Then take time to pray for these specific needs or requests.

Chapter Nine

GET RIGHT WITH OTHERS

One of my friends, Jerry Craig, was a fairly new Christian. He had a deep love for the Lord and a love to share his faith with other people. He was also faithful in attending services and digging into God's Word. After about six months passed, he seemed to cool off. He began to lose the joy of his salvation and it troubled him.

One night Jerry and his wife asked Carolyn and me over for dinner. We had a wonderful meal. Then Jerry and I went off into my photography darkroom to work under the enlarger and to talk about things in general.

We sat down in the darkness with no other light on except the darkroom safe light. Jerry said, "Preacher, I have a problem. I do not know what is the matter. I have searched my heart. I have read the Word, but everything is just dry. I do not want it to be this way."

Now read very closely because someday you may be in this same state if you are not already there. It is like an airplane that quits flying. Those of you who are pilots know that when you are flying a light plane and you pull that stick back and it quits flying, the plane just settles in. You lose air speed.

As a Christian sometimes you go gangbusters, and then all of a sudden, you just seem to settle in. You come to church, you are faithful, perhaps you even teach a Sunday school class, but you have lost the joy of your salvation.

"Well," I said, "Jerry, sometimes God wants to teach us not to depend upon emotion. God is not an emotion. Do not treat him like an emotion. Feelings come and go. Sometimes emotions depend on what you ate last night. Emotions fluctuate. This is caused by human physiology and human chemistry and psychological factors and the weather and who knows what else."

"No, it is more than that," Jerry replied.

"All right," I said, "let's begin to look. Is there any known sin in your life?"

"Well, I cannot think of anything," he replied. "Of course, I sin every day, but I have tried to keep short accounts with God."

I said, "Well, dear friend, I do not know exactly what is wrong, but as a babe in Christ, God will tolerate some things in your life that as you begin to mature he will not tolerate any longer. You know a mother and dad will tolerate things in a ten-month-old child that they will not tolerate when he is ten years old. Perhaps there are things in your life that God expects you to deal with at your new level of maturity."

I asked, "Is there any bitterness in your life?"

"No," he said, "I am not bitter with anyone."

I said, "What about bitterness in the past?" Well, I could not have made any more impression on him if I had hit him with my fist.

He said, "Oh! Well, I had not thought about that. I have an uncle whom I have hated for years. Now that I think about it, I still feel the same way."

I said, "All right, you are going to have to treat your uncle and those feelings toward your uncle just as Jesus treated you. He forgave you out of pure grace—undeserved favor. In the same way, you are going to have to forgive your uncle. Now tell me about your uncle."

Jerry explained, "Well, when I was just a child, my father and my uncle went into business together. For a number of years, the business prospered very well. Then, because it had prospered so well, my uncle pushed my father out of the business with a shrewd move. My uncle went on to become very, very wealthy. After that, my father made a decent living, but it was always difficult."

Jerry continued, "Our family was angry, and I have always been angry toward my uncle."

I asked what he thought he ought to do about it now. He grinned and said, "Well, let's take it to the Lord." We did.

I then asked Jerry, "What now?"

Jerry replied that his attitude was right toward his uncle. I asked him if his uncle still knew that he was bitter, and he replied, "Yes." I then asked him what he thought he needed to do.

"I believe I will write him," Jerry said. So Jerry wrote his uncle a letter:

> Dear Uncle Ben,
>
> I have had a bitterness in my heart toward you for many years. But because of a new relationship that I have with Jesus Christ, he will no longer tolerate the attitude that I have had toward you.
>
> I want you to forgive me for my bad attitude toward you.

Notice that he did not ask his uncle to repent. He did not condemn his uncle for what he had done. That was not Jerry's responsibility. Jerry's responsibility was to make his attitude right toward his uncle.

We have the tendency to say that we will ask forgiveness if the other person will. We may want to wait until the other person says he is sorry or until the other person makes some kind of restitution. Jesus gave us the command to forgive others as he has forgiven us. Then he gave us a model to follow on the cross. Even when he was being killed by an angry mob, Jesus prayed, "Father, forgive them; for they do not know what they are doing" (Luke 23:34). Following Jesus' example, we need to forgive others without conditions. When we release others, we can know the cleansing and forgiving work of God in our lives as well.

Remember, God is always the initiator of reconciliation. You show me a life where God is full and free and at liberty, and I will show you someone who is a reconciler.

Jerry immediately received a glowing letter back. However, the response does not matter. What matters is if you have done what God asked you to do.

Jerry's uncle wrote, "Oh, Jerry, I cannot tell you how I have grieved over this misunderstanding over the years, but I have not known what to do about it. This relationship you have with Christ is very interesting."

Jerry wrote his mother and asked when Uncle Ben's birthday was. That October Jerry sent Uncle Ben a birthday card and received back another tremendous letter.

Jerry was so excited. At Christmas he sent Uncle Ben and Aunt Martha a Bible, but Jerry did not receive a word back. January passed, and I asked Jerry if he had heard from Uncle Ben. He said, "No, I believe I blew it."

I will never forget Jerry's excitement as we were preparing for a sweetheart banquet at the church on February 14. He came sailing in, grabbed me, and said, "Pastor, I have to tell you something. I received a letter from Uncle Ben today." Then he handed me the letter. It said,

> Dear Jerry,
> Sorry I have been so long in thanking you for the Bible, but I felt I should read it first. And you will be happy to know that after reading this Bible, I now have a relationship with Jesus Christ just like yours.

Remember: every time you begin to cross swords with someone, whether it is at business or home or wherever, perhaps God has engineered circumstances between you and this person in your concentric circles because he wants you to be a channel through which He can love and reach down and meet a person's need. People are frustrated, they are angry, they have all kinds of problems and resentments, and they need you.

GOD'S CONDITIONS FOR RELATIONSHIPS

There are two basic types of relationship in life. The most important relationship we have is the vertical relationship we have with God the Father. The only way any of us can come to the Father is on his conditions.

The other basic type of relationship is the horizontal relationship we have with other people. God has laid down the basis for all of our other relationships. Accepting his conditions for relationships means that we forfeit forever the right to choose whom we love. The kind of love we will express has nothing to do with looks, age, shape, size, color, sweetness, hostility, or personality. Anyone Jesus chooses, we will love.

In relationships—marriage, business, or any interpersonal relationship with anyone—we must accept Jesus' lordship. When Jesus becomes Lord of our lives, he is going to draw people into our circles who will not be lovely. Jesus said that any sinner can love any other sinner—not because of human love but because his love can flow through us to anyone he chooses to love through us.

Having accepted God's conditions in establishing a relationship with him, you then must accept his conditions for establishing horizontal relationships with people. If your relationships with others are broken, the flow of God's Spirit is hindered or stopped.

GOD WORKS THROUGH RESTORED RELATIONSHIPS

As God begins to use a person, he begins to knock down walls of resistance and bad attitudes in that person's life. Perhaps some relationships in your own life have not been made right. God wants to use even those relationships for his glory.

Often, the first thing that comes to mind when we think of confessing a ruptured relationship is: *If I am a Christian and I admit I have been wrong in an attitude or whatever, what will the other person think of me?* That is pride raising its ugly head. Who cares what the other person thinks of you? What does God think of you when you are acting in obedience to get a relationship right? Look at what the person will think of Jesus if you do not make the relationship right.

Are there ruptured relationships in your life? Matthew 5:23–24 says that even if your brother is upset with you, go to him and be the reconciler. Because you are the one who is living in victory, you are to be the reconciler.

So keep your conscience clear. If the Holy Spirit brings something to your mind that is wrong in your life, set it straight. Deal with it. Keep short accounts with God and with others. What we need is a personal revival, a personal walk, letting the Lord work out his redemptive purpose in and through our lives.

Sometimes I meet people who have difficulty with concentric circles because they do not want to reconcile relationships in those circles. But it is impossible to be right with God and wrong with those around us. Would you be willing to sacrifice a right relationship with God over any human relationship you have? If you would, then you really do not know God the way he wants you to know him. Nothing could be more valuable than being right with God.

Friend, your world needs you. People all through your concentric circles need you. Be a channel of God's love. There is no greater thrill in life than letting the Lord love through you and meet needs through you. That is the Christian life.

I can tell you hundreds of stories about students with ruptured relationships with their parents who have led those parents to the Lord. Now they have a liberty and a freedom because the ruptures are cleared. Get right with others in your concentric circles, and God's love can flow through you to see their lives forever changed for God's glory.

PERSONALIZING CHAPTER 9

Using a journal or notebook, respond to the following questions or activities. Record details that will help you understand and apply the truths of this chapter to your own life.

1. We've talked about broken relationships throughout this book. Do you have any relationship that you have been refusing to reconcile? Now is the time to get right with others. Without doing so, you cannot get right with God. With an unclear conscience, you will not be able to get a balanced view of self either. Ask the Lord to enable you to take the actions necessary to be reconciled with others—all others. Then begin taking those actions.

2. Have you allowed pride to affect any of your personal relationships? If so, humble yourself and be reconciled to those you have offended by your pride.
3. Do you need to write a letter, make a phone call, or better yet, make a visit to an "Uncle Ben" in your life? Go ahead now and obey the Lord. Let God set you free from bitterness, unforgiveness, or guilt over a broken relationship.

BUILDING UP THE BODY

This is a critical turning point in your study together. Group members need to experience victory over their relationships with others. You can help each other, pray for each other, and encourage each other.

Use the following questions and activities with your small group to help one another apply these truths to your lives and to build up the body of Christ.

1. How has God recently guided you to get a relationship with another person right? What did you do? How did the other person respond? As people share testimonies, take time to thank God for obedience, cleansing, and victory. If people have not responded in a positive way to these actions toward reconciliation, pray for them. Pray also that the Lord will bless and honor the obedience of the one who is seeking reconciliation.
2. In what broken relationship are you still struggling to seek reconciliation? How can we pray for you in this relationship? What can we do to help you?
3. Discuss ways you may be able to help each other in getting relationships right.
4. Ask each small-group member: *How can we pray for you this week?* Then take time to pray for these specific needs or requests.

Stage 2

*S*urvey:
*S*urvey *Y*our *R*elationships

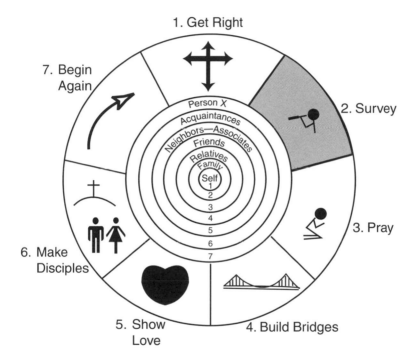

STAGE 2 SUMMARY

SURVEY YOUR RELATIONSHIPS

Many people who have been Christians for a long time may not think they have relationships with people who are lost. We don't stop to think about all the people that God brings into our lives or into the circles of our influence. I've found that when people begin to identify the people in their concentric circles in a survey, they find all kinds of people who need the Lord.

I will guide you in identifying people in your circles of influence and in recording basic information that can guide your praying, bridge building, and loving. First we'll look at those closest to you in your immediate family and your circle of relatives. Then we'll start identifying your friends, neighbors, business or school associates and acquaintances. I will also help you think about the "Person X" people that God may bring across your path. This survey will become a prayer list for you to begin praying for those God has brought into your concentric circles.

Chapter Ten

Survey Circles *2* and *3*: Family and Relatives

Jeff's brother had left home in the late sixties with the hippie movement. His family had not seen him since.

Jeff told me about his brother, saying, "He has broken my parents' hearts. We do not know if he is dead or alive. I am not sure I want to know what has happened to him. Can I leave him out of my Circle 2?"

"No, Jeff," I answered. "God put your brother in your circle for a reason. Write his name down in your survey. Intercede for him. Get your attitude right toward him."

As Jeff met God's conditions of relationship toward his brother, he received a deep burden to pray for him. Months passed and nothing happened. But Jeff was faithful and continued to pray. Then all of a sudden, an inexplicable, unexplainable circumstance arose that drew this brother to Fort Worth. He called Jeff. Jeff called me at 2:30 A.M. after he had talked with his brother.

"Dr. Thompson, are you awake?"

"Well, I am now," I laughed.

Jeff then explained, "Dr. Thompson, this is Jeff. My brother just called. I have been praying and here he is. He is coming to class with me in the morning."

"Good," I said, "tomorrow I will teach the class how to come to know Jesus in a personal way." And I did! And he did! Jeff's brother accepted the Lord in my office after class.

I want to tell you something. When you get things right in your own life with God, He will begin to engineer humanly impossible circumstances to bring more people into your concentric circles to have their needs met. God can bring more people than you could ever run down on purpose. You become fulfilled as you see the fruit of God's Spirit impacting the lives of those around you.

97

WHY A SURVEY?

You may ask, "Why is a survey necessary?" For the simple reason that you cannot remember everything you need to remember without writing it on paper. You need a structure for your evangelism. Nothing ever becomes dynamic until it becomes specific. As you take your survey, you become conscious of people that you never would have thought of. They are in your circle and perhaps in no one else's.

A pastor friend of mine presented the concept of concentric circles to his church. The people began to make their surveys and to pray. In one month, the church had sixty professions of faith. So, do a survey. It is important. It is the structure upon which you build.

Remember, as you do your survey, your lifestyle is not only loving the lost but also the saved. Your concentric circles will contain many people who are already saved. Do you pray for them? I hope so! They have needs and hurts too. Meeting their needs becomes a part of your lifestyle. Showing God's love to them is a place for you to practice loving others the way God wants you to love the lost world.

SHAKING THE FAMILY TREE

As we move beyond the Self and Circle 1, we make a survey of Circle 2 and list the members in your Family. Here I list Carolyn, my wife, and Damaris, my daughter. Because my father has gone to be with the Lord and I am the only son, I also list my mother in Circle 2. I am in constant contact with her. These three constitute my Family.

Your Family will include those who live under your roof. If you are away from home and not married, your survey for Circle 2 will include your mother and father. If you are married, your Family will include your spouse and children. The rest of your Family will go under Circle 3, Relatives. We will discuss your survey of Relatives later in this chapter.

If you are not the channel of God's love to meet the needs of those in your Family, forget about reaching Afghanistan for Christ. We get concerned about the ends of the earth, yet often we cannot meet the needs of our own families.

Love is meeting needs. If I am not allowing God to use me to meet my family's needs, my evangelism becomes hypocrisy. No wonder we do not want to share the gospel with the whole world. If it is not real at home, it is not going to be real out there either.

Now you ask, "What does this have to do with evangelism?" Everything. God has given the home as the context in which we learn to build relationships.

HOME: THE TRAINING GROUND

Let me illustrate. I have many students who come to me weeping and say, "Dr. Thompson, I did not do very well in high school. I did not do very well in college. I want to go into the ministry. I want to study Greek and Hebrew, but I did not do very well before. But now I am going to do my best."

I do everything in my power to help them, to encourage them. But this is the tragedy. Those students do not have a solid background in the school of knowledge. They have not taken seriously the tools they were given on which to build the rest of their lives. Education is a discipline. Education is an opportunity to learn how to use your tools. You then use these tools the rest of your life. You can start building that foundation later in life. However, you've wasted some precious years, and making up for lost time becomes more and more complicated the longer you wait.

The same principle applies to relationships. If you blow the opportunity of learning how to use the tools of relationship that God has given you in the home, then you have blown everything.

What are you going to do? As you move through your circles, you find a child who is in trouble with the police. He has already been in trouble with himself. He is not free with himself. So he is in trouble with his parents. He is in trouble with his teachers. He is in trouble with God. He is in trouble with everyone because he did not learn right relationships in his home. If we do not use the home as the basis for building relationships, we have lost our tools. Now, God can do much to make up for lost years and learning experiences, but you miss out on God's best.

FINDING YOUR KISSING KIN

Circle 3 includes all Relatives. That circle can go on almost indefinitely. You may say, "I do not know most of my family." Well, shake the family tree. You will be surprised who will fall out. You will find people you never thought of, but you have a relationship with them that is blood kin or marriage kin. That puts them in your line of relationships.

List the names of these relatives. Get as much information about them as you can. Fill out a survey sheet for each one. The key is to let God guide you in identifying their needs. Then all you have to do is show an interest and a love for people. They will turn to you and say, "Oh you care!" Listen, people, that is living! Love is meeting needs.

But you say, "Good grief, I have a zillion relatives! You mean I am supposed to pray for all of them?" You may even think of giving up.

I realize that you cannot pray for each relative every day. But write the names of all your relatives on your survey sheets in your notebook, and then during your quiet time, flip through your survey sheets, sometimes just looking at names.

Do you remember Susanna Wesley? She was John Wesley's mother. She had nineteen children in twenty-two years. She was a very busy woman. To take care of everyone, she had to organize very carefully. Once she was asked which of her children she loved most. She replied, "The one who is hurt at the moment." Do you know why? Because of their needs. Love is meeting needs. As you move through your relatives, you will begin to know who has needs at that particular time. God may cause you to become aware of needs as your invitation to join him in his work in their lives. It's very important to be close to your family.

GREAT AUNT ALICE

One of my friends was working through his survey of Circle 3 and remembered his great aunt Alice. Dick had met Aunt Alice several times at family reunions, but he was not even sure where she lived. He wrote his mom and said, "Mom, where is Aunt Alice? I have her on my prayer list. Can you get her address for me?"

Dick's mother wrote back and reported that Aunt Alice was eighty-two years old and in a rest home about eighty-five miles from where Dick lived. She sent him Aunt Alice's address. Then on Aunt Alice's birthday, Dick sent her a birthday card.

Aunt Alice wrote back, thrilled to hear from him. After several weeks, Dick called her to set up a time when he and his wife could drive out to visit her.

Dick introduced his wife to his Aunt Alice, and they talked about the pleasantries of the day. Then Aunt Alice asked, "Well, Honey, tell me what you do?"

"I am in Southwestern Seminary studying for the ministry," Dick answered.

Then Aunt Alice asked, "Well, what do you study?"

Dick replied, "Basically, I study that the most important word in the English language, apart from proper nouns, is *relationship*. Like the relationship we now have. I also study that if you really love someone, you meet his needs."

"Oh, that really sounds interesting; tell me more," Aunt Alice said.

"Well," Dick replied, "the basic need in the life of every individual is to know Jesus Christ in a very personal and intimate way."

"That sounds very interesting," she said. "Please tell me what you mean."

He then shared with her the gospel: how a person comes to know the Lord, how to have sins forgiven, and how to live in a right relationship with the Father and with those about him.

Aunt Alice looked at Dick, big tears filling her eyes, and whispered, "Son, I have been a member of a church for years, but I have never done that. Could I trust Jesus?"

Dick said that he and his wife knelt down beside that dear little lady at that moment, and she invited Jesus into her heart. When I saw Dick months later, he came up and put his arms around me. He could not talk at first because he was kind of choked up. But he hugged me and said, "Doc, this weekend Aunt Alice went to be with the Lord."

Then he added, "Dr. Thompson, what if I had not listed her in my concentric circles? What if I had not done my survey?"

I do not want to lay a heavy burden on you, dear reader, because God wants you to take one day at a time. So redeem the time. Use it. You cannot win all of your family in one day. You have the rest of your life, however long that may be, to work through your concentric circles. Be available to God. Allow God to love through you to meet people's needs. Live under God's grace and strength. Remember Colossians 2:6. As you received Christ by faith, walk with him by faith.

PERSONALIZING CHAPTER 10

Using a journal or notebook, respond to the following questions or activities. Record details that will help you understand and apply the truths of this chapter to your own life.

1. Prepare a database for your survey. Choose one of the following formats to maintain your survey:
   • Notebook: Photocopy the survey form on pages 204–205 and have it punched to fit into a three-ring binder. If you prefer, use a computer to customize your survey form. Make many copies so you will have one for each person in your survey. You may want to start with thirty or forty sheets, though I've known people who

end up with hundreds of people in their survey. Save a master for copying when you need more survey sheets. Use tabs to separate the forms into the Concentric Circles 2 through 7.

- Journal: Using a notebook with writing paper in it and the survey sheet on pages 206–207 as a model, record the information you need for the people in your concentric circles. If you can rearrange the pages, you can keep the survey sheets for each circle together. If you cannot rearrange the sheets, mark the circle in the top corner of the page or use a color code so you can identify the circles for each page.

- Computer Database: If you have a computer, use one of your programs to maintain the database for your survey. You might choose a card file and keep an index card for each person in your survey. You could keep a separate file for each circle. Another option would be to use a database program, a worksheet program, or just a word processing program. In any case, use the survey sheet on pages 206–207 as a model for the information you will keep on each person. You could prepare a template of the form so you only have to fill in the blanks.

- Index Card File: Using a box for large index cards and the survey sheet on pages 206–207 as a model for the information you need, prepare an index card for each person in your survey. Use tabs to organize your survey based on the concentric circles.

2. Begin compiling a more detailed survey of everyone in your concentric circles. Right now focus on Circles 2 and 3, Family and Relatives. Use a separate survey sheet or card for each person.

- First, prepare a sheet for each person in your immediate family. This includes all the people who live in the same home with you (parents, spouse, and/or children). If you are single living away from home, include your parents. Include as much information on each person as you have available. Add to this as you find out more of the information that may be helpful to you.

- Next, prepare a sheet for each relative. This list will grow over time. Start with those who are closest to your immediate family. Include all relatives who do not live in the same house with you and who are not in your immediate family. Include all the relatives you can think of or those with whom you have any relationship. Think about:

grandparents	parents	brothers	sisters
stepparents	in-laws	aunts	uncles
grandchildren	nieces	nephews	cousins

3. Once you've prepared surveys for these two circles, take some time to begin praying for each person in your survey. Ask the Lord to begin revealing their needs. Ask him to teach you how to pray for and show love to each one. As you pray for each person, record on your survey sheet any insights the Lord may give you.

4. Before you move on to the next chapter, ask yourself: Have I knowingly omitted anyone from these two circles because of a broken relationship? If so, go back and add that person. Give that relationship to the Lord and ask him what you need to do next.

Building Up the Body

Use the following questions and activities with your small group to help one another apply these truths to your lives and to build up the body of Christ.

1. How have you chosen to maintain your survey information (notebook, journal, computer files, index cards, or other)?

2. If some in your group have prepared computer templates for their files, they may want to share copies with others who would prefer using a computer for their surveys.

3. What special insight, if any, have you gained about the people in your immediate family? Have you prayed in a special way for them that has proven to be especially meaningful? How?

4. Which relative in Circle 3 have you added to your survey who seemed to surface unexpectedly? Have you experienced any unusual circumstances this week related to these relatives that seem to heighten your awareness of them?

5. Have you knowingly omitted someone from one of your circles? How can we pray with and for you concerning that relationship?

6. Of those in your survey, which one do you sense God might put at the top of his "Most Wanted" list for you? Ask him: Take some time for each person to tell about their "Most Wanted" person, and pray as a group for each of these people. Begin asking the Lord to engineer circumstances in their lives through which he will draw them to salvation.

7. What have you done or experienced in the past week as a result of our study thus far? How is God working in your relationships?

8. Ask each small-group member: *How can we pray for you this week?* Then take time to pray for these specific needs or requests.

Chapter Eleven

Survey Circles 4-7: From Friends to Person X

Driving from Houston one night, Carolyn, Damaris, and I were listening to the CB radio. If you have one, do not be afraid of it. If you know only ten or twelve words, you can use a CB. I enjoy talking on it and never know whom I will meet.

My handle is not Sky Pilot or the Preacher. With those names, some people would not talk to me. So mine is Jelly Bean. With that handle, I talk to everybody.

It was late that night, driving from Houston, and I was tired. I was talking on the CB to help keep myself awake. Damaris had settled down on the back seat. We had cleared the city, and the chatter had died down. No one else was saying much so I started talking to a fellow called Rocky Mountain.

I asked him, "What is your home 20?"

He answered.

"Where are you going?"

He replied, "San Antonio."

We talked on a little more. Then everything grew silent.

After a while, Rocky Mountain said, "Jelly Bean, I am going to San Antonio to see a preacher. If that preacher cannot help me, I am going straight to hell!"

Damaris, who was almost asleep in the back seat, came over the seat and said, "What did he say?"

I said, "Friend, I know that you are going to find this hard to believe, but Jelly Bean is a preacher."

He said, "Jelly Bean, a preacher!"

I answered, "That's right, and I would be happy to talk with you." To make a long story short, at the next easy-on, easy-off service station, I pulled off and climbed into the car with him. In fifteen or twenty minutes, he invited Christ into his life.

You never know. You just never know where they are. The Holy Spirit just draws them. They are there. They are hungry. They are hurting, but they sense the world does not care.

You see, I will never see Rocky Mountain on earth again.

He came in and out of my life like a comet. There are many people you will never see again. But God holds you responsible. He wants you to be available.

Just before his ascension into heaven Jesus said to his disciples: "You shall receive power when the Holy Spirit has come upon you; and you shall be My witnesses both in Jerusalem, and in all Judea and Samaria, and even to the remotest part of the earth" (Acts 1:8).

You have a Jerusalem—those closest to you. You have a Judea—a broader concentric circle. You have a Samaria—a still broader concentric circle. And you have a remote part of the earth. Someday the Lord is going to ask, "What did you do with them?"

Now you say, "Father, I cannot meet the needs of the whole world, but I can meet needs in my own world." Do you hear me? "I can love my world. I can meet needs in my Jerusalem. And then Lord, you may have to drop some bombs in my life, but you will push me out into Samaria and the uttermost parts of my world."

You cannot give out of your own resources and meet all the needs God brings into your life—they are not sufficient. However, you can give out of Jesus' resources. God plus you always equals enough.

SURVEYING CIRCLE 4: CLOSE FRIENDS

Our close friends are in Circle 4. Sometimes close friends are closer than relatives. Include in this list the people you spend time with, the ones you talk to about important things, the ones you participate with in hobbies or recreation activities. These are the people you could call in the middle of the night if you needed help, and they would gladly come. Friends who are not as close can be included in Circle 5.

Close friends have needs too. Do not forget to meet them. Don't just wait to receive from your friends. Watch for ways God may invite you to show his love by meeting their needs. If they are believers, you get to practice "love one another." If they are unbelievers, pray that God's love through you will be used to draw them to Christ.

Surveying Circle 5: Neighbors and Associates

Circle 5 includes neighbors, business associates, classmates at school, and not-so-close friends. Remember, it is so important to write down the information about them on your survey sheet. Why do you want to do this? Because you care. You find out about people you care about, don't you? Let me illustrate.

When someone asked how I met my wife, Carolyn, I answered that at the time I was the twenty-seven-year-old pastor of First Baptist Church in Sequin, Texas, unmarried, "unseminaried," and "un-everything" else. I had gone through Baylor University but had not found a wife.

A dear friend, a Methodist layman who loved God, called one day and asked me to come by his office. He wanted to talk to me about visiting a family with a Baptist background.

Passing through his outer office the next day, I met his private secretary. Guess who? Carolyn. There she sat as I stumbled over the chair and the wastepaper basket and knocked the phone off the desk as I was going from one door to the next.

When I finally made it to my friend's office, he handed me a sheet of paper with the family's name on it. "But wait," I said, "we will discuss that family later. Who is that beautiful creature?" I spent the next three weeks conducting an investigation like the FBI. I wanted to know everything I could about that girl. Then I planned my strategy. Now she is my wife!

Listen friend, when you care and God wants to care through you, you will want to know about people. So make your survey.

Getting to Know Your Neighbors

In the city it has become an increasingly greater problem to know our neighbors. But if love is meeting needs, and if we want to meet our neighbors' needs, we must know them.

My neighbors will not believe that I want to be in heaven with them if I do not want them in my home for dinner, or if I do not say hello when we are in our front yards together. We have to know our neighbors before we can meet their needs.

A friend of mine lives across the street from a Korean couple. They are very quiet, and developing a relationship with them has been difficult.

My friend said that after months of trying to build a relationship, there was a death in the couple's family. The wife's mother died. My friend and his wife took the Korean couple a meal. They took care of their animals and mowed their yard. When the couple came home, they said to my friend, "You have been so kind. We would like to be your friends."

Now these friends are ready to listen to the gospel from someone who has shown them love. Love is meeting needs wherever we are.

However, I want to remind you that if you are going to take your world for Jesus, you must have a new, fresh, and uncluttered love for our Lord. You and I must be more "self-forgetful."

Several years ago, when I was so near death, I learned something from the Lord that I will never forget. I learned that it is not how long I live; it is how I live. Methuselah lived 969 years and may have died in the flood of Noah's day. So what? Enoch, his father, lived only 365 years. "And Enoch walked with God; and he was not, for God took him" (Gen. 5:24). Which would you rather be? Let God guide your living so that your life will count for him and be fulfilling for you.

SURVEYING CIRCLE 6: ACQUAINTANCES

Moving from neighbors into Circle 6, you ask, "Who is an acquaintance?" Well, have you ever been in a grocery store or a restaurant? Do you remember seeing those little name tags worn by the checker or the waitress? Those are not there just for decoration. They bear the names of people who are your acquaintances. We know their faces, and as Christians, we really need to be sensitive to their names as well.

When you call a waitress, do not say, "Hey, you!" One of the deepest needs of any individual is recognition. One way to give recognition to a person is to call him or her by name. It means something to call a person by name. It means that you value him and are concerned enough to remember his name. Remembering a name may not seem like much, but it means you care. You meet a need every time you say a person's name. Back in the Garden of Eden, when God was looking for Adam and Eve, God did not say "Hey, you!" He said, "Adam, where are you?"

You may say, "I am not good at names." Let me be a little harsh with you. If you do not remember names, it is because you do not care enough. Remembering names takes time. You really have to work at it. I encourage you to work at it!

As you begin to work through your concentric circles and it becomes a lifestyle, you will begin to realize how important names are. When you call acquaintances by name, they will never forget you.

I know some preachers who cannot preach their way out of a brown paper sack. They are like dump trucks, but they cannot dump. They are loaded with knowledge and information. Some of them are overloaded. They just do not know how to share it. But let me tell you something. They know how to love—to meet needs; and God uses them. People love them. Why? Because it is difficult not to love someone who loves you.

Now what about children? Is remembering their names important? Yes! It lets them know you care. There is the story of the little boy who, hearing his father pray the Lord's Prayer, misunderstood the words. When the little boy repeated the prayer, he said, "Our Father who is in heaven. How did you know my name?"

In your survey, list your acquaintances in Circle 6. Get as much information about them as you can over a period of time. Then, as you build those relationships, you will learn their needs.

SURVEYING CIRCLE 7: PERSON X

Finally we come to Circle 7, which contains Person X. "Ah," you say, "you have talked about everybody else, but you have not talked about that lost world out there."

Friend, that lost world out there is all we have been talking about. Why? Because somewhere out there in somebody's circle, your Person X may be listed. You see, your Person X may be in my Circle 3. My Person X may be in your Circle 2. To me, some of you are Person X's.

What did Jesus mean in Acts 1:8 when he said "You shall be My witnesses both in Jerusalem, and in all Judea and Samaria, and even to the remotest part of the earth"? Just what was he saying to me and to you? Well, to the apostles, their world was first Jerusalem, then Judea and Samaria, and finally the remotest parts of the earth. They started where they were and moved out.

He is telling us to go to our Jerusalems, our Judeas and Samarias, and outwardly expand. We are to start where we are.

My world is not your world, and your world is not my world. But if we all put our worlds together, we can take the whole world! Do you know what I have discovered? When God is filling me with his Spirit, he has ways of drawing people into my circles.

You will not be able to develop a survey sheet on most of your Person X's in advance. These are more likely to be people who cross your path for the first and perhaps only time. You must be praying and prepared to love them and meet needs. Once you have had an experience with a Person X, complete a survey sheet so you can remember to pray for that person. Include all the information you know. You may not even know the names of all the Person X's who come into your life, but you can describe them sufficiently to remember to pray. Who knows, you may cross paths with that person again. God may begin to move a Person X into a closer concentric circle over time.

TAKE YOUR TEMPERATURE

Some of my students say, "I never see anybody who is lost." But I tell them, "You had better check your spiritual thermometer." I have found that God has a way of drawing people into my circles when I am walking with him. They just materialize, and I see them.

If you love everyone in your circles, you will find there is a "holy magnetism" through your life. God will draw people through you to him. Remember, love is meeting needs.

Also, let us remind ourselves that when we think of evangelism, we must not think only of Person X. We must think of our whole world, of all our concentric circles.

One day, a student sailed into class after we had discussed concentric circles.

"Dr. Thompson!" he exploded.

"What's the matter?" I answered.

"Guess what! I just met someone out here who is a Person X. She is a blond, and she is beautiful!"

I asked, "And?"

"I want to bring her into my Circle 2."

"She may not want to come," I said, "but I will pray for you."

Remember that God will bring people into your Circle 7, and they may then pass through like a comet. They are related to you only for a moment, but God puts them there for a purpose. You may never see them again. John 7:38 assures that "from his innermost being shall flow rivers of living water." If I am walking in the Lord and in agreement with him, I am living. His living water will flow through my life and through others in the process.

God says, "Here is one of my children. I can bear fruit in his life." So God draws someone into the life of his child, knowing that he will meet the needs of Person X. When Person X is touched by a child of God, that person receives power.

Remember when Jesus was walking through the crowds one day? They were jostling him on every side, shoving and pushing and eager to press in upon him. Suddenly Jesus turned and asked, "Who touched my garments?" (Mark 5:25–34). His disciples could not understand and asked Jesus what he meant since many people were touching him. But Jesus answered that somebody had really touched him, and he had felt power leave him. Then a little woman standing nearby confessed that she had touched him. Through his power, she was healed. She was a Person X, and Jesus met her need.

PERSON X NEEDS YOU

Dear friend, someone is going to "touch" you. Maybe it will be someone on an airplane, like the Hollywood producer I met, someone with a need. It may be on a train or a bus. But when people touch you, do they touch God's power? Do they encounter his living water? And will you take the time to meet the needs of that Person X?

Do you understand what I am saying? People will pass in and out of your life. You may never know when to expect them. Be ready. Pray, "Father, here I am." He knows who needs loving and will put that unknown person into your Circle 7. Sometimes God brings a person into your life in an irritating circumstance in order to test your response to his grace.

Some of my students who formerly had not been able to find lost people will admit, "You know, when I am walking in submission to my Lord, I accidentally bump into more people who need Jesus than I ever could run down on purpose." This is God bearing fruit in their lives as they become aware of and meet the needs of Person X.

What is your spiritual temperature? Are you walking closely to the Lord? Do his life and love flow through your life? Is he able to bring people into your life knowing that they will encounter Christ there?

We must remember to include Person X who, like a comet, comes into our lives only for a moment and then passes through. We may never see him again, not in this lifetime. He may touch us only for a moment. Will he touch power?

Do you know what I have realized? The person who has right relationships has the power of the Holy Spirit not only resident within his life but also moving through his life as well. The Holy Spirit is always resident in a Christian. But when he is allowed to be free, he is constantly moving in and through your life to meet needs. You may call it the fullness of the Spirit or a great unction of God that is upon your life; call it whatever. Just remember that the Holy Spirit will engineer circumstances to bring Person X into your life, knowing that you will be faithful to love him and to meet his needs.

PERSONALIZING CHAPTER 11

.Using a journal or notebook, respond to the following questions or activities. Record details that will help you understand and apply the truths of this chapter to your own life.

1. Using the format (notebook, journal, computer file, etc.) that you adopted for your survey, continue surveying your concentric circles. Prepare survey sheets on:

   • Circle 4: Friends—those you spend time with and really care about, trust, and can depend on for help in times of need.

   • Circle 5: Neighbors and Associates—people you know and have some sort of ongoing opportunity to interact with on a fairly regular basis. Consider the following:

neighbors	coworkers	supervisors	union members
vendors	clients	subordinates	
classmates	teachers	fellow church members	
students	teammates	fellow club members	

   • Circle 6: Acquaintances—people you "bump into" occasionally, usually for short periods of time. However, you can get to know them better than a Person X of Circle 7. Consider people you meet at or in:

grocery store	gas station	restaurant	club
school	church	party	store
mall	government	association	sports events

   • Circle 7: Person X—people who only briefly cross your path unexpectedly. They may be people you will never see again. God may point you to add to this circle someone you know of but have never personally met. This would be a person with whom you would begin building a relationship bridge. It may be with a person you meet once and want to continue praying for, like the Hollywood director described in a previous chapter.

2. Keep in mind that your survey will grow over time. Add as many names to your survey as you have time for or God leads you to take time for. Let your survey become more of a lifestyle than a one-time project.

3. Take some time to pray through the people you have listed in your survey. Ask the Lord which one or ones are on his "Most Wanted" list for you. Begin making these persons a special matter of prayer.

Begin watching for ways God will work through you to show love to them or build deeper relationships with them.

4. Before you move on to the next chapter, ask yourself: Have I knowingly omitted anyone from these circles because of a broken relationship? If so, go back and add that person. Give that relationship to the Lord and ask him what you need to do next.

BUILDING UP THE BODY

Use the following questions and activities with your small group to help one another apply these truths to your lives and to build up the body of Christ.

1. What special insight, if any, have you gained about the people you have added to your survey this week? Have you prayed in a special way for them that has proven to be especially meaningful? How?

2. What persons have you added to your survey that seemed to surface unexpectedly? Have you experienced any unusual circumstances this week related to these people that seem to heighten your awareness of or involvement with them?

3. Did you knowingly omit someone from one of your circles? How can we pray with and for you concerning that relationship?

4. Of those in your survey, which one(s) do you sense God might put on his "Most Wanted" list for you? Ask him! Take some time for all the members of the group to tell about their "Most Wanted" person(s) and pray as a group for each of these people. Begin asking the Lord to engineer circumstances in their lives through which he will draw them to salvation.

5. What have you done or experienced in the past week as a result of our study thus far? How is God working in your relationships?

6. Ask each small-group member: *How can we pray for you this week?* Then take time to pray for these specific needs or requests.

Stage 3

Pray: Work with God Through Prayer

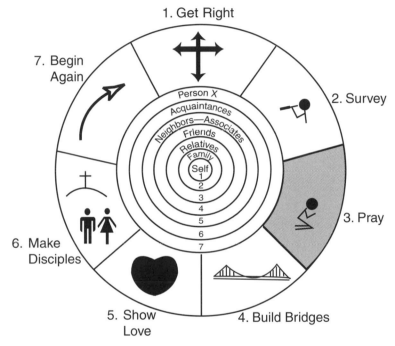

1. Get Right

7. Begin Again

2. Survey

3. Pray

4. Build Bridges

5. Show Love

6. Make Disciples

Person X
Acquaintances
Neighbors—Associates
Friends
Relatives
Family
Self
1
2
3
4
5
6
7

STAGE 3 SUMMARY

WORK WITH GOD THROUGH PRAYER

Prayer is not just a religious activity you go through before you begin your work for the Lord. Prayer is a relationship with the Master of the universe. When you pray, you enter the throne room of heaven where the decisions that govern the universe are made. God invites us to pray so that when he answers we will know he did it. He will get the glory.

I will help you learn to pray for wisdom and discernment as you seek to make disciples. You will learn to pray for God to engineer circumstances in the lives of others to draw them to himself and to his Son Jesus

Christ. You will pray about the people in your survey and watch to see where God is working in their lives. When you become aware of needs, that will be your invitation to join God and show his love to the needy person.

Chapter Twelve

WORK WITH GOD
THROUGH PRAYER

A lady by the name of Alice came to our church. Her husband's name was John. Because the ladies in Sunday school built relationship bridges and reached out to Alice, she came to know the Lord.

Then Alice became concerned about her husband and said to me, "Please pray for John. He has never been in a Protestant service in his life." Well, in a few weeks John came quite reluctantly to his first Protestant service. It scared him to death. Do you know why? He was under conviction. He did not know what was going on. He had heard the gospel and realized that something was missing in his life.

Six fellows in our church manned our SWAT (Spiritual Weapons and Tactics) team. Paul said, "The weapons of our warfare are not of the flesh, but divinely powerful for the destruction of fortresses" (2 Cor. 10:4). We believed God had given us powerful spiritual weapons that could break down the strongholds in people's lives. One of those powerful weapons is prayer. These men on our SWAT team knew how to intercede, and they knew how to build relationship bridges to people.

I gave them John's name, and they descended with gusto. They began to pray for him, and they began to love him. They took him to lunch and played tennis with him. They knew he needed Christian fellowship.

One day John went home and laughingly told Alice, "Honey, those Baptists are after me." Well, he liked the attention, but it also frightened him because he was under conviction of sin.

Each of the men on the SWAT team came to me and said, "Pastor, I do not understand. I have tried to confront John with the very essentials of the gospel, but I am having difficulty."

I responded, "Keep praying. God has something in mind." You know, intercessory prayer is like a guided missile. It always hits its target. Here was our prayer for John. "Father, you engineer circumstances in John's life to draw him to you."

John continued to come to the services every Sunday, and we continued to pray. This went on for a couple of months.

By this time, John had come to love the fellowship of our people, but he was so under conviction that he was miserable. So what did he do? He joined the National Guard. By doing that, he would miss services two Sundays a month.

John's decision was quite a shock to Alice, and she was so discouraged. I said, "Alice, you just pray that you will be the kind of wife that John needs and love him. That is your responsibility. Do not try to be the Holy Spirit. God knows what he is about."

Often when we begin to pray, circumstances do not go the way we would have planned them. Sometimes they really get tough. But do not let that alarm you. Who is bigger—God or the problem? You see, the Lord knew John better than we did. Through all of these circumstances, God was working.

One day, when everything had seemed to go badly for John, he walked across a rental yard talking to a fellow about renting a truck. John turned the air blue with profanity as he complained to the fellow about everything.

"John," this other fellow said, "I want to tell you something. I used to be under pressure like you are until I gave my life to Jesus Christ."

John hushed. He got into the truck and drove away. The fellow had not confronted him with the gospel; he had just gently shared a brief personal testimony.

The next day was Sunday and Guard day. John was relieved that he did not have to go to church. Walking across the parade grounds, talking to one of the other sergeants, again he complained about everything.

All of a sudden, this other fellow said, "John, you know, I used to feel that way. I was in such a turmoil until I gave my life to Christ."

John thought, *Good grief!* He was a photographer for the Guard. He went into the darkroom, closed the door, kind of sighed, and said, "Oh, it is good to get out of that bright sunshine and into this darkness."

But there, working under the enlarger, was a guy who quipped, "Well, you know what the Scriptures say, John, 'men loved the darkness rather than the light; for their deeds were evil'" (John 3:19).

Pow! There is power in prayer. There is no human way this whole scene could have been arranged. The whole plan came from a living, loving God. What was happening? A sovereign God was answering prayer and engineering circumstances to draw a life to himself. That is the work of the Holy Spirit.

John went home and said to Alice, "Honey, it is not just those Baptists. Christians are everywhere!"

The next week he came charging past the receptionist, past my secretary, and into my office. Closing the door to my office, he announced, "Preacher, I am in trouble!"

"What's the matter?" I asked.

"I am going to get a divorce!"

"You are going to do what?"

"I am going to get a divorce!" he repeated.

"Why in the world would you want to do that?" I asked him. "You love that woman!"

He said, "I cannot give spiritual leadership to my home."

And I said, "Brother, I have heard many reasons for divorce, but this is not one of them." It was a weird conversation, but this is just the way it went.

"I know what you are going to say," John grumbled. "I know you are going to say that I need to trust Jesus."

"You said that," I told him.

"But that is what you are going to tell me," he repeated as he turned and walked out of my office.

I started to follow him, but the Holy Spirit said, "No, everything is under control. It will be all right."

John got back into his truck and headed toward Dallas. Somewhere on the turnpike between Fort Worth and Dallas, he stopped his truck, got out, knelt down pretending to change a tire, and said, "Lord Jesus, save me."

Later that afternoon, John came back to my office. "Signals check," he said and smiled. "Everything is all right. Now I can be the spiritual leader in my home." And off he went.

The Holy Spirit had convicted John of his condition before God. You see, you can convince people, but it takes the Holy Spirit of God to convict. My convincing someone only makes him feel guilty, but when a person is convicted by the Holy Spirit, he can see that he is held in high treason against heaven's King.

Let me share with you something else. Some people are very difficult. You think they are impossible. They will not come to church, and you think, *If I cannot get them to church, how in the world can they be saved?*

The truth is that people can be saved inside and outside the church. First-century Christians were saved without a church building. Sometimes we think erroneously that the only place someone can be saved is inside the church building. When we join God in his work through prayer, the all-present God can touch people anywhere they are and draw them to himself. Intercessory prayer is the first and greatest step you need to take in reaching out to lost people with the gospel of Jesus Christ.

THE GREATEST WORK—INTERCESSION

The one indispensable ingredient in a great church and a close walk with God is knowing how to pray. But real prayer is more than "cliché praying": asking God to bless the meal or praying before a Sunday school class or pulling the alarm of prayer in a time of trouble.

ONLY IN CASE OF EMERGENCY

When I was a little boy, my family would go from our home in Gonzales, Texas, to San Antonio for the day when my daddy was going to sell cattle. I stayed with my mother and two sisters while my dad did his work.

I learned from those early experiences that shopping with women is not easy. They wanted to look at everything on God's green earth. It was terrible, especially for a four- or five-year-old boy.

Finally, after the ladies had finished their shopping, we would wait for my dad at our meeting place in the lobby of the Gunter Hotel. I would be tired and fretful after all that shopping, but I did not want to sit and wait. So my sisters, Laurel and Nelwyn, would take me for walks. While we walked, I had questions about everything. One day on one of these walks, I saw a big red box on a pole with a glass window in front.

"What's that?" I asked.

"That's a fire alarm," Nelwyn answered.

I saw the little hammer hanging by the box. I listened as my sister explained to me that if a fire emergency occurred, someone would take the hammer, break the glass, pull the fire alarm, and then the firefighters would come. The idea really fascinated me.

Remembering this incident caused me later to make a comparison. Red letters beneath the box read KNOCK OUT GLASS *ONLY* IN CASE OF EMERGENCY. Many people have a prayer box, which they use much like the fire alarm. Only in case of an emergency do they really get earnest about prayer. If you are not in the habit of praying, it is usually too late to learn when the crisis comes. You are not spiritually prepared to pray if you are not in the regular practice of prayer.

I have heard that preventive medicine is better than dealing with a disease after you get it. We could prevent much tragedy in our hearts and lives—as well as in the hearts and lives of our children, our churches, our concentric circles—if we continually prayed for each other before tragedy hit.

Often we wait until our child stumbles and gets into trouble or becomes a problem, or we wait until someone gets desperately ill or we see a marriage going on the rocks. We do need to pray with intensity at times of emergency, but wouldn't praying constantly, like Paul did, be much better? He said, "Pray without ceasing" (1 Thess. 5:17). We need continually to pray through our concentric circles and trust that a sovereign God is working through circumstances to draw people to himself. Keep in mind that he wants them to be saved more than you do. That is why he has called you to work with him to "make disciples" (Matt. 28:19).

The life of the apostle Paul was saturated with prayer. If you read carefully the life of our Lord Jesus, you will understand that his life was also permeated with prayer. If we think we are going to make it without praying, we are badly mistaken. No wonder people are not converted and lives are not changed. People are not taking prayer seriously.

If you do not believe in a supernatural God, you will be in trouble because you will think, *I am going to have to manipulate this whole thing!* You try, but you may get your hands burned.

Believing in a supernatural God does not mean you become passive and do not do anything. No, you are moving; but while you move, remember that you are God's instrument. The direction comes from him. Your job is to intercede, to pray for people, and to meet needs.

PRAYING FOR WISDOM

Paul showed us how to intercede. He said, "This I pray, that your love may abound still more and more in real knowledge and all discernment" (Phil. 1:9). Paul was praying for the Philippians to have wisdom and insight to meet people's needs through their love. Have you ever prayed Philippians 1:9 for anyone? Have you ever prayed for God's wisdom to meet another person's needs?

When you pray, pray for wisdom. You may ask, "Holy Father, give me wisdom to deal with this person." God will give it. When you pray for wisdom, do not sit around waiting to feel wise. Begin to move. As you are going, God will supply the wisdom. "If any of you lacks wisdom, let him ask of God, who gives to all men generously" (James 1:5).

Sometimes we parents say, "I want to love my children. I want to meet their needs." But sometimes we unwisely get wants and needs confused. If we meet all their wants, we hurt them. There is a difference between meeting wants and needs.

We are like the little girl who found her kitten out in the rain. Because she loved it so much, she did not want it to catch cold. So what did she do? She stuck it in the oven and turned up the heat! We do not doubt her sincerity, but what about her wisdom? As parents, we desperately need godly wisdom.

PRAYING FOR WISDOM FOR OTHERS

My Damaris is in high school now. She is becoming a beautiful young woman. I pray for Damaris's wisdom. She has many temptations now and is making many decisions. As the father of an only child, I am trying to hold her and to shove her at the same time. If I hold her too tightly, she will never grow. Only godly wisdom can help me know the proper balance in holding and letting go.

I do not know how long I will be in this clay house. None of us know. We need to pray now that our children will have wisdom. We need to pray now that we will have wisdom to instruct them.

I must pray that Damaris will be sensitive to the leading of the Holy Spirit. So I pray, "Father, give Damaris wisdom to make the decisions she needs to make today." Do you know what I have found? When I am praying for her, I do not fuss at her. I find that my temper is not as sharp, I am not as frustrated with her when she does dumb things (just as I have done and still do dumb things), and I see her come through with a blaze of wisdom.

I also pray daily for that young man she may marry some day. I pray that God will prepare him to be the right kind of man and that God is teaching him wisdom as he grows and matures.

Now, you may think that I have fallen off the lowest limb of a tree and hit my head, but if I have, just leave me in my befuddled state. I like it because I can sense what God is doing, and I can see my prayers becoming reality. God is moving. He is directing and leading. Remember, before we can pray effectively for others, we have to be right with the Lord. We have to take Self (Circle 1) before the Lord and clear out the sin in that circle; then we can get down to business on Circles 2 through 7.

God holds us accountable for everyone who comes into our concentric circles. He wants us to love people and intercede for them. Remember that love is meeting needs.

HOW DO I INTERCEDE?

PRAY IN SPECIFICS

Do not pray in blanket form. You know, "Lord, bless them all." Too often we come to God and say, "Lord, just bless us." No! God expects us to pray for specific things. Sometimes we do not want to pray specifically because we are afraid that God might not answer specifically. If you do not pray specifically, as we have learned in James 4:2b, "You do not have because you do not ask," then how will you ever know if God answers prayer?

Move through your whole family. As you begin to intercede for these loved ones in Circle 3, and later for friends in Circle 4 and so on through the whole survey, you will need to be sensitive to the Holy Spirit's leadership to those who are in the deepest need. In time, you are going to find several hundred people in your survey. There will be aunts and uncles and kinsmen you never dreamed were there.

God will help you to know when he wants you involved with a particular one. When you become aware of a need, that may be your invitation. When you are praying, you may sense a special burden to pray for a particular person. You might just call or write to that person and see what may surface because of that contact.

A PRAYER PATTERN

Do you want to intercede for others? Then let me suggest a pattern for your prayers:
- "Lord, make me a clean channel for your love."
- "Give me godly wisdom."
- "Father, you engineer circumstances in their lives to draw them to you. Create circumstances where I can love them and meet their needs."
- "Lord, make me available."
- "Lord, make me aware of their needs and show your love through me as I seek to meet their needs."

- "Give me boldness to confront them with your love and with your message of forgiveness."

That is the way you intercede. Then you do loving things. Some people may not respond to you in love. Do not expect everybody to love you back immediately. Sometimes people do not know what to do with your love because many people in your world have never really been loved. Consequently, when you do something loving toward them and meet their needs, they may wonder, "What does he want?"

Regardless of how people respond to you, just keep loving. Be genuine, and do not expect too much too quickly. Make yourself available to God as he leads. After a while, others will learn that you really care. Meet their needs, and ask God for wisdom as you work with them.

Now that you have done your survey and you are interceding, you and the Lord must work out how you intend to divide your circles to pray for the people. Since there are seven days in a week and you have seven circles, you may want to take a circle a day or a long and short circle each day. It does not matter as long as you have a plan. As you pray, ask the Lord to reveal to you the needs of those in your circles. He is more interested in your prayer time than you are.

As we intercede and ask for wisdom, we also ask God to engineer circumstances to draw people to him. Sometimes it gets cloudy and dark when we start doing this. Sometimes a crisis comes, but do not let that alarm you. Sometimes darkness increases before the light breaks through. Sometimes it is a desert for months. But keep loving as you keep praying.

REACHING OUR FAMILIES

Some of my students have great difficulty working through Circle 2 and Circle 3—their families. They say they do not want to pray for Mom and Dad because of bitterness between them, perhaps even about coming to the seminary. Many students want to come to the seminary and go directly to Circle 7, maybe to Africa or somewhere else around the world to share the word of Jesus. But they do not want to pray for some of those people in their inner circles.

We have ruptured relationships, but God says that when Jesus becomes Lord of our lives, we must surrender forever the right to choose whom we will love.

I once told a class: "Now you are responsible for building bridges, interceding for your families, and making sure that you meet their needs." If you are going to bear the character of Jesus Christ, you are going to have to love, and love is meeting needs.

FINDING A MISSING BROTHER

I had one student come to me and say, "Dr. Thompson, when my brother got into the drug culture two years ago, things really got bad at home, so he left. He wanted to do his own thing. He was addicted, probably selling it, and everything else. What should I do? I love him, but I feel so helpless. I do not know how to find him."

"Well, that is no problem," I told him. "God knows where your brother is."

Sometimes we pray like, "Father, I do not know if you can do this or not." But when you intercede for someone, it is like a guided missile. It is instantaneous. And it is on target. There is no defense.

That student began praying for his brother. One day the student came into my office and said, "I received a call from my brother. He has been converted and is going home."

My student almost sounded disappointed because he did not get to witness to his brother. But let me say this. He was ready to witness to him; his heart was right with God and through his intercession, his brother was freed to choose the Lord. Prayer is Kingdom work just as much as sharing a verbal witness.

PENETRATING PRAYER

Someone once told me, "My brother will not get within a hundred yards of a church. We cannot reach him. You try to talk to him . . ."

"Dear friend," I said, "you can pray for him. He cannot resist prayer because God breaks down those walls and barriers. You pray, 'Father, open his eyes to his spiritual condition and set him free. Lord, engineer circumstances in his life to draw him to you.' It will thrill you to see what God will do if you pray and make your life available."

We have a sensational God. He deals and specializes in the impossible.

You must intercede for those in your circles. You must pray for God to meet their spiritual, physical, or whatever needs they have. You are his vessel. You must be available.

Another student who had graduated was back on campus several months ago. Entering my office, he laid his ragged concentric circles notebook in my hands.

"Dr. Thompson, here is my notebook," he said. "I want you to look at it."

That young man—who had never led anyone to the Lord before—in one year, had led to the Lord thirty-eight people listed in his concentric circles. Can God do that? Yes, and he can do that through your life. Are you willing to begin working with God in prayer? Are you willing to make your life available to show the love of God to others by meeting needs?

A SMALL-GROUP PRAYER PLAN

Can you imagine what would happen if all your Sunday school classes or cell groups used concentric circles as their outreach program? First, each person would do a survey, then he would begin to intercede every day. Intercession is not a "Dear Lord, bless me and my wife, my son John and his wife, us four, no more," and jump into bed. No, each person would genuinely intercede by surrounding others with prayer. Intercession would become a lifestyle. Ruptured relationships would be righted. Walls would have to be torn out and new educational buildings built to hold everybody!

NANCY AND HARRY

Carolyn accepted the invitation to lead an adult ladies class at the church I was pastoring. This class had just never made it. With about twenty-five on the class roll, its average attendance was three—two plus the teacher.

The Lord gave Carolyn a heavy burden for this class. She knew that God wanted her to take it. One afternoon she brought home the class roll. Of the twenty-five names on the roll, she knew only five. Carolyn decided that what these ladies needed most at this time was intercession. So an hour or so each day that week she prayed for all twenty-five members. Then she invited to our home the four members who attended occasionally.

Carolyn laid out to the four members this plan: Each person, including Carolyn, would take the names of five women who were on the class roll and pray for each one daily. The ladies agreed. They were not to contact the other women, just to pray for them. Now they had a plan. Nothing becomes dynamic until it becomes specific.

Since we had been at the church only a few weeks, Carolyn asked if the women knew the others on the roll. Some they knew, but some they didn't.

All four ladies seemed to be familiar with Nancy, who was on Carolyn's prayer list. All four ladies warned, "Do not try to visit Nancy. She and her husband, Harry, are very bitter toward the church. Harry will slam the door in your face. He may even be dangerous to someone from the church. They have been hurt and are very bitter."

Carolyn thanked the ladies for their advice but reminded them that the Lord specializes in cases like this one and that he loves this family. She said, "We will pray that the Lord will engineer circumstances so that we can love them and meet their needs."

About three weeks later, an aide from the hospital who attended Carolyn's class called Carolyn saying that Nancy was in the hospital with pneumonia. Carolyn and one of the class members went to visit Nancy. They took her some flowers.

Nancy was appreciative. The class member with Carolyn offered to take care of Nancy's children while she was in the hospital. Nancy really appreciated this help because she did not know how they were going to manage. Finally, Carolyn and the other woman left their phone numbers in case there was anything else they could do.

The next day Nancy called Carolyn to say that her husband had been brought to the hospital. He had fallen and injured himself. Carolyn and I immediately went to the hospital to meet Harry. When we walked into his hospital room, he beamed with appreciation for the ladies' help. Instead of an angry, bitter man, he was just like a big, old teddy bear.

The next week, when Nancy and Harry went home from the hospital, the Sunday school class took food to them. Nancy and Harry didn't throw the women out this time. They were so grateful. You see, all they needed was God's love to flow through God's people to them. It is difficult to fight genuine love.

God did not cause the sickness or the injury. That is not how he operates. But he allowed it to happen so that Nancy and Harry could see the love of God. He had prepared their hearts to accept us.

Nancy and Harry and their two children were in Sunday school and church the next Sunday. They very rarely missed anything at the church from that time on. God does answer prayer. The question is: Do we care enough to intercede?

After the experience with Nancy and Harry, and after the four ladies had prayed for their five ladies, a love began to develop within these women that made them want to meet needs. They began to reach out to these families in love. One by one, these women began to come to Sunday school. They were in a concentric circle. They had a contact. They knew they would walk into the class, and the one who had reached out to them would be there.

One of the four ladies was concerned with a lady we will call Jan, who not only was having mental problems, but also family problems. Jan came to Sunday school regularly for five weeks. One day after class, Jan came to Carolyn and said, "I just want you to know that I will be out of town next Sunday. We are going to visit my family out of state." As Jan talked, Carolyn wrote her name and phone number on a slip of paper. She handed it to Jan, and Jan put it in her purse. In two or three days, Carolyn received a phone call from the hospital. Jan had taken an overdose of sleeping pills. When the ambulance had come, Jan told the driver to get the sheet of paper from her purse and to radio for Carolyn to come to get the children at her house. She said she did not know whom else to call.

A lady in Carolyn's class began to intercede for Jan. Jan was able to begin to deal with her own problems as Christ became real in her life. Within six months, she was able to begin reaching out to meet other people's needs. She and her husband were reunited, and they took vital roles in the church.

In only three months the class had at least twenty-five members present each Sunday and had to find a larger meeting place in the assembly area. From their survey, their intercessory prayers, and building bridges, within seven months the class averaged thirty-five to forty women each Sunday. That is what can happen when a Sunday school class gets really serious about concentric circles—about loving—about meeting needs—about intercession.

WHAT ABOUT THE CHURCH?

Can you imagine what would happen if all the members of a church began to take surveys of their concentric circles, to intercede, to reconcile all relationships, and to show love to those in their concentric circles? We would go into the worship service expecting and anticipating God's working in hearts and lives.

Dick, another of my students, was called to pastor a little country church. It was one of those situations where the church had been there forever, and the members planned to remain there forever. But they did not plan to do anything.

When they were looking for a preacher, usually a seminary student, they hired him if they liked him. Then, if they changed their minds, they would fire him.

Dick said, "Dr. Thompson, what should I do? I preach, but nothing happens. I want them to pray, but they do not want to. They say they hired me to pray. I want them to go visiting, but they do not want to go visiting because they say visiting is my job. These people could take the heart out of a hickory log. They do not want to do anything. But, they did want to have a 'meetin'.'"

I know the word is *meeting*, or *revival*, but they wanted a "meetin'." So I said, "Dick, why don't you share concentric circles with them?" He did.

After his presentation, one of the deacons said, "Preacher, I have a son who was married in this church last summer. He and his bride have not been back since. I had not even thought about it. I am going to put them down in my circles and pray for them."

Then a little grandmother came up to Dick and said, "You know, I have a granddaughter who is fourteen. She has never made a profession of faith. I am going to pray for her."

Several others told Dick that the message had reminded them of someone to pray for.

Well, this little church had its "meetin'." They also had seventeen professions of faith, which doubled the size of their congregation! The people were so excited that they kept adding to their survey.

These who once could have taken the heart out of a hickory log were interceding, building bridges, confronting people, and learning what the word *disciple* means. This is revival. These people had caught the vision of their Jerusalem, their Judea, their Samaria, and their world and how the gospel moves through concentric circles.

Senior Adults, We Need You

Churches need to mobilize retired people, shut-ins, and senior adults to pray. Because they have more time to pray, they can provide a powerful ministry in our churches.

Over the years, I have had shut-ins and retired people pray for me. How thankful I am for them. While I was at Baylor University, a dear little saint prayed for me. At the time, I had a church in Gonzales, and I drove back to Baylor late every Sunday night.

"My husband has already gone to be with the Lord," this dear lady explained to me. "I am here alone and have much time to pray. I am going to pray for you each Sunday night until I know that you are back in the dorm."

One night, just out of Round Rock, north of Austin, I came upon a terrible wreck. I was the first person on the scene and offered to help. I was delayed several hours. So I did not get in the dorm until about 4:30 A.M.

The next weekend I went home to my church. The dear lady who promised to pray for me called, asking, "Where were you Sunday night?"

"What do you mean?" I asked her.

"You kept me awake until 4:30 A.M. praying for you," she answered. God would not let her go to sleep until I was safe.

Those of you who are up in years, listen to me. You say, "There is not much I can do anymore." But do not tell me that because it is not true. Until Jesus calls you home, you can provide the most profitable time of all your life in intercessory prayer. Why not link yourself with some young families who are having problems? Do not interfere—just pray for them. Become their "prayer umbrella." Find out about some of the young people who need prayer—all of them need prayer. You can become a vital part of their lives by praying for them.

Also pray daily for your pastor, your church, and the other staff members. Pray for our president, our country. There are battles to be won in prayer. Become intercessors. That is what we need. Oh, how we need you.

Just go through your concentric circles and pray for your Jerusalem, your Judea, your Samaria, and your world. Praying will change your life as much as it changes the many lives of those you are praying for. Meeting their needs will allow God to meet yours.

PERSONALIZING CHAPTER 12

Using a journal or notebook, respond to the following questions or activities. Record details that will help you understand and apply the truths of this chapter to your own life.

1. Consider dividing your survey sheets into smaller groups so you can pray more specifically for each person in your survey. Depending on how large your survey is, you may want to divide it into seven groups and pray for a group one day each week. Or divide it into thirty groups and pray for one group each month. At the same time, develop a list you pray for every day—your "Most Wanted" list. This would include your immediate family as well as those few people God has given you a very special burden to reach.

2. Now, using your survey, begin to use this prayer pattern as you pray for yourself and for each individual. Use the topics listed below, but expand them by being more specific as the Holy Spirit guides your

intercession and petition. You may want to copy this list on a card as a guide until it becomes second nature to you.

- "Lord, make me a clean channel for your love."
- "Give me godly wisdom."
- "Father, you engineer circumstances in their lives to draw them to you. Create circumstances where I can love them and meet their needs."
- "Lord, make me available."
- "Lord, make me aware of their needs and show your love through me as I seek to meet their needs."
- "Give me boldness to confront them with your love and with your message of forgiveness."

BUILDING UP THE BODY

Use the following questions and activities with your small group to help one another apply these truths to your lives and to build up the body of Christ.

1. What unique, unusual, or especially meaningful experiences have you had this week as you have prayed for the people in your concentric circles survey?
2. In what ways have you seen God begin to answer some of your prayers?
3. Discuss the SWAT (Spiritual Weapons and Tactics) team idea at the beginning of the chapter. Would you have people in your church who would sense God's call to be part of such a team? Talk with church leaders if you believe God is giving you an invitation to start such a team for the people in your church's concentric circles of concern.
4. Discuss the small-group prayer plan mentioned in this chapter. Is this a plan God would want your small group or class to use in praying for the people related to your group? If so, pray and ask the Lord to call out a volunteer who would coordinate the plan. Then take some time at each meeting to pray together as well as to report on what God is doing in answer to prayer. If members need to help each other in meeting needs to show love, discuss ways you can help each other.
5. What have you done or experienced in the past week as a result of our study thus far? How is God working in your relationships?
6. Ask each small-group member: *How can we pray for you this week?* Then take time to pray for these specific needs or requests.

Stage 4

Build Bridges: Build Relationship Bridges to People

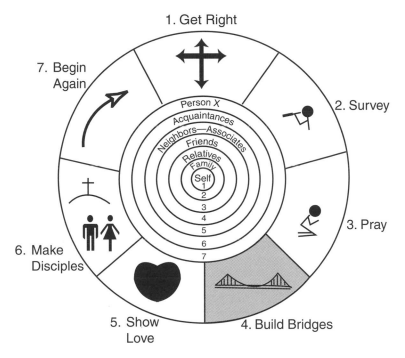

1. Get Right

2. Survey

3. Pray

4. Build Bridges

5. Show Love

6. Make Disciples

7. Begin Again

Person X
Acquaintances
Neighbors—Associates
Friends
Relatives
Family
Self
1
2
3
4
5
6
7

STAGE 4 SUMMARY

BUILD RELATIONSHIP BRIDGES TO PEOPLE

Sometimes your relationship with people in your concentric circles is so shallow or distant that you have little way of reaching out to them in love. At other times, you will become aware of a person who needs the Lord and you will intentionally begin building a relationship bridge to that person so that God's love can flow to him or her.

You can build relationship bridges to people in a variety of ways. You can show an interest in them during special times of joy or times of stress. You can build bridges through shared interests or hobbies. You will find that building bridges is not a waste of time. When people come to Christ through existing relationships with Christians, they are far more likely to follow through in establishing a growing relationship with a church—probably the church you attend.

Chapter Thirteen

BUILD RELATIONSHIP BRIDGES TO PEOPLE

One of my friends told me a story that happened when he was a young boy. One night he came home and saw his dad really working on something. Jim said, "Dad, what in the world are you doing?" His dad replied, "I am working on this telegraph key, learning the Morse code."

"Why?" asked Jim. "You are not interested in ham radios."

"Yes, I am," his father replied. "You know Greg Smith's father down the street, the house with the big antenna?"

"Yes," Jim answered.

"I tried to reach him, but he would not even talk to me," Jim's dad replied. "The only thing he knows and loves is ham radio. I am going to learn how to be a ham radio operator so that I can reach Greg's dad."

Jim's dad took the time to build a bridge to Greg's dad. The bridge was a ham radio. Six months later, Greg's dad trusted Jesus. That is reaching out in your concentric circles and building relationship bridges.

Now that you have done your survey, begun to intercede, and made yourself available to God, you will want to build bridges to people by reaching out in love and showing them that you care.

UTILIZING POINTS OF CONTACT

What is building bridges? It is simply meeting needs in a person's life or showing an interest in him or her in such a way that a relationship is established. It may be a gentle touch or a smile. You show me someone who intimidates people, and I will show you someone who is intimidated. You show me a servant of God, and I will show you someone who is always loving and meeting needs.

What is the purpose of a bridge? It is a structure that makes crossing over from one side to another possible. To us as Christians, building a bridge is building a relationship that lets us cross over into the world of another. When we have crossed over into this person's world, he or she feels safe, and the time will come when the person will feel comfortable in crossing over into our world. It is a continual process. It is the process that makes a relationship.

The apostle Paul sought to build relationship bridges for the cause of the gospel. He said:

> For though I am free from all men, I have made myself a slave to all, that I might win the more. And to the Jews I became as a Jew, that I might win Jews; to those who are under the Law, as under the Law, though not being myself under the Law, that I might win those who are under the Law; to those who are without law, as without law, though not being without the law of God but under the law of Christ, that I might win those who are without law. To the weak I became weak, that I might win the weak; I have become all things to all men, that I may by all means save some (1 Cor. 9:19–22).

Do you see why Paul built relationship bridges to people? He wanted to see them come to salvation in Christ. Paul tried to identify with the needs and lifestyles of individuals around him so that he could lead them to Christ.

Building relationship bridges should be a continual process in your life. It should become a part of your lifestyle. The closer we are to the Lord, the more person-oriented we will become. Continually building relationship bridges to our family, relatives, friends, neighbors, associates, acquaintances, and even to Person X's is a significant part of life. Not only do bridges allow you to share Christ with others, but they allow you to experience more of the abundant life Jesus came to give you. Relationships are important

Doing something like sending a birthday card may be a great way to start your lifestyle of bridge building, but it is only a start. The process is a continual one. We should utilize as many points of contact as possible in bridge building. We need to become experienced master bridge builders.

When you begin to sense that God wants you involved with a particular person, begin to look for points of contact. Ask yourself: *How can I touch this person?* If you do not have a point of contact, create one. The challenge is to build bridges so that you can begin to converse with a person about things that interest him.

UTILIZING POINTS OF CONTACTS

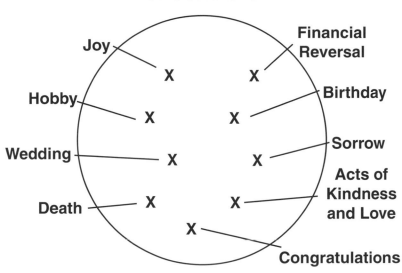

MAKING A POINT OF CONTACT

As you meet people, find out where their interests are. Then talk with them about the things that interest them. Like Jim's dad at the beginning of the chapter, you may have to develop some new interests or become knowledgeable in a subject in order to reach out to a person.

I have a contact point with Jews because I am partially Jewish. Some time ago in Houston, I met a Jewish man who was a motel desk clerk. He asked me, "Where do you work?"

I replied, "I am interim pastor at the Baptist church down the road."

"Oh," he said, "I am Jewish."

And I said, "Oh, I am too." He looked at me questioningly. I asked, "What tribe?"

"Pardon me?" he replied.

"What tribe?" I repeated.

He answered, "I am not sure. What is yours?"

I said, with quite a bit of pride, "The tribe of Judah. I will be back next weekend. Maybe you can find out this week about your tribe. We can talk more about it next week."

It is important to utilize our points of contact. We need to get on the wavelengths of those in our concentric circles by building bridges and establishing relationships. Building relationship bridges to people is a continuing and rewarding process.

What are the best times for building bridges? Rejoicing when others rejoice and providing support in times of stress are good times to build relationships.

BUILDING BRIDGES DURING TIMES OF JOY

HAVING A BABY

One way to touch people's lives is to show them attention and consideration at the time of the birth of a baby. I have stood in a hospital and looked through the glass at some beautiful, little horrid faces. Do you know what I mean? You tell the parents how beautiful their baby is. There are beautiful babies, and there are beautiful babies who are not beautiful. I think if ever there is a time when God forgives us for lying, it is at the birth of a baby. How many times I have stood at the baby window in the hospital with a couple. What a wonderful, warm time to build a bridge!

We all laugh at the crazy behavior of fathers when the time comes to go to the hospital. I remember Carolyn telling me at about 10:30 one night, "Honey, I think we had better go to the hospital." Well, we went. As they asked us questions at the nurses' station, I could not think of my name, Carolyn's name, or our address. But they all knew me at the hospital, so one of the nurses escorted me to the nearest chair. Then she asked Carolyn the rest of the information. I thought Carolyn was going to have the baby before they finished getting the information. But Damaris was not born until the next afternoon at 1:37. There is no other time like the birth of a baby.

I have talked with new fathers as we both stood looking through that glass window at a precious little life. At times we have talked about the overwhelming responsibility of being parents. I tried to emphasize, "That is a great little life. Do you realize that God has given you the most important gift you will ever have?"

Gifts and cards can be ways to express your interest during the birth of a baby. But the things that make the greater impressions are the personal expressions of interest. Visiting in the hospital shows far more interest in the individuals you are seeking to build a bridge to than just sending a card.

When mother and baby go home from the hospital, think about ways you can express your interest by meeting a need. Take a meal so the new mom doesn't have to cook. Clip a birth notice out of the local paper, laminate it, and send it with a note. Send some flowers to add some cheer, or volunteer to baby-sit one night so the new parents can get a little break from the action.

WEDDINGS

Another good time to build bridges is at the time of marriage. Reach out and be helpful. When parents are helping a first child marry, they are going to need help. If you have been there before, you could offer suggestions that may save quite a bit of time and wasted effort. You might tell them about the special offer of a free wedding planner at the department store when the bride registers there. Tell them about the free CD with wedding music samples that is available at the local Christian bookstore. Watch for ways to show your interest—like clipping and sending the wedding announcement from the paper (or even collecting extra copies from friends so they can send copies to relatives).

Pastors and staff members, do not miss this opportunity to build bridges. The more your church can do to provide help for the family and the new couple, the more you may be able to show the love of Christ to them. You might even prepare a "So You're Getting Married Kit" with all the helpful tips you've learned by helping couples in the past. Help make the experience as easy and pleasant as possible.

Pastors, be sure to counsel couples before the marriage. You may tell the couple, "This is one of the most important decisions you will ever make. Therefore, it is imperative that you know some of the things that will make you happy."

Through the years as a pastor, I have told couples in our counseling sessions before their marriages, "For a marriage to be whole and all that you want it to be, all of the parts of the puzzle must fit." I believe that the key to a successful marriage is intimacy. When you think of intimacy, you usually think of physical intimacy, but there is much more to it.

To have a biblical marriage, intimacy must exist on three levels. *Mental-emotional-intellectual intimacy* is the first. Intimacy at this level means that no one on the face of this earth is closer to you than your mate. Do you want your marriage to be in trouble? Then let someone other than your mate get closer to you. If you depend on someone else more than you do your mate, if you want to share all of your deep thoughts with someone else more than you do with your mate, then there is a problem.

If you do have a problem in your marriage, take the first step. Begin to communicate. Talk about every problem, and do not let resentment and pride build up. Count the costs. The stakes are high because your marriage is in the balance. But when communication is flowing and warmth and love are present, two people cannot be happier. This kind of bond cannot be broken.

I can share with Carolyn when I cannot share with anyone else. Even though my daughter and I are very close and have a very special relationship, it is different from the relationship that Carolyn and I share. Someday I want Damaris to have this same kind of very special relationship with her husband, and I pray that there will be no closer person on the face of the earth than those two are to each other.

Second, a biblical marriage must have *spiritual intimacy*. You are a spiritual being. Marriage is a holy triangle between a man, a woman, and God with God's love flowing through the man to the woman and from the woman to the man. It is a forgiving, redemptive, sharing kind of love.

The key word in marriage is *intimacy*. If you have a problem, discuss it. Be open. Be mature. Work through your problems. Until a couple really communicates about a problem and works through it, that same problem will flare up throughout their married life. Take your problems to the Lord. Nothing is too big to be worked out at the foot of the cross.

The third level is *physical intimacy*. All three levels of intimacy are essential to a strong, fulfilling marriage. If there is a problem in one of the first two levels of intimacy, physical intimacy will not be all it should be. Some people marry only for physical intimacy. When it ceases to satisfy, they move on. They will never find lasting fulfillment without all three levels of intimacy.

Intimacy comes through a relationship. Sometimes I say to couples, "I am not as interested in your church membership as I am in your success as a married couple. Your attitudes toward your marriage and the basis upon which you build your marriage are going to make the difference in whether you succeed or not."

For a marriage to be all it needs to be, both husband and wife need to have a close relationship with the Lord. Your spiritual intimacy with each other is based on your relationship first of all to Christ and then to each other. Any other way, your relationship becomes selfish: me, my, and mine.

The results of this selfishness are seen in many marriages. One or both persons may say, "I will stay with you as long as you make me happy. As long as things go well, as long as we have money, I will stay with you.

As long as you meet my needs, I will stay." Those of you who have experienced the agony of divorce understand what I am saying.

When do we start teaching concepts of intimacy to children? We start at birth and demonstrate to our children what a marriage should be.

If you are a pastor, you need to preach what a marriage should be, what God intended it to be. When I pastored, I talked to my teens quite often and would tell them, "All right, you lovebirds sitting back there holding hands, I want your attention." Of course, I had it. "If you are planning to get married, I do not want you to plan two weeks before and then come to me and say you have to set a date. No! I want you to start planning now."

Do not make fun of puppy love. It is real to the puppy! If young people start building unreal relationships, what they call love, and misunderstand love, they will never establish the type of relationship God has in mind for them.

So often young people start with intimacy on the physical level. Then they wonder why this physical relationship does not satisfy. They go from one physical relationship to another and never find the fulfillment they are searching for. They miss God's plan for intimacy between two people.

One night a teenage couple came into my office and told me they were in love. The fellow was very belligerent and did not want to talk in the first place. He was not a Christian. The girl was a wonderful Christian.

I said, "I want to be perfectly blunt with you, Ann. If you marry Billy, you will not be marrying a whole man. Billy is not all there."

Billy looked at me quite shocked. All of a sudden, he was interested in everything I said. I continued, "Ann, you are going to be trying to build a whole marriage, and you are a Christian. You say you hope someday he will be, but he is not. He does not have the equipment to make you totally happy. Oh, a week or two, a couple of years, but he just does not have it."

Then I turned to Billy. "You see, Billy, there is a part of you that is absolutely dead. You are thinking me, my, and mine right now. You are not thinking of this girl. At this point, you two could never experience spiritual intimacy together. There would be a void in your marriage."

After the shock of his realizing his condition before God, I explained the plan of salvation to him. He trusted the Lord.

Remember, I really had been telling the truth when I had said that Billy was not a whole man. He was not all "there" until he had a spiritual dimension. When that part of his being became alive, he became a whole person. I was not calling him a half-wit; I was just not calling him a whole-wit.

Two people need to have all three dimensions of intimacy balanced in a Christian marriage. Until they do, their marriage is a "hope-so" marriage and not a sure thing.

BIRTHDAYS

Sending birthday cards is another important way to build bridges. A birthday is a very special day. Teachers, if you want to build bridges to your students, this is a beautiful time to do it. Send them birthday cards. You say, "Oh, that is time-consuming." I know, but it really makes a difference.

Also, think about your business associates, a business partner, your business contacts, your colleagues, and employees. Send them birthday cards. Build bridges.

When I was interim pastor at MacArthur Boulevard Baptist Church in Irving, I sent birthday cards to every member. I sent out many cards each week. My secretary at the church would address and stamp them, but I would write a little paragraph and sign each one.

What a thrill when I stood at the back door of the church after the service and the little children would come by and hug my neck and give me a "moisturized" kiss that went from ear to ear and say, "Thank you for my birthday card."

CONGRATULATIONS

Showing people that they are special to you is building bridges. Suppose you want to reach teenagers. If they win district in spelling or a football game, or if they do something special that you read about in the newspaper, then cut the notice out of the paper, circle it in red, and write on it, "That's great. I am proud of you." Sign your name and send them the clipping. You will have an open door into their world. Build bridges to these people in your concentric circles.

OTHER TIMES OF JOY INCLUDE:
- congratulations
- promotions
- expressions of appreciation
- graduations
- anniversaries

I remember one of my first pastorates. It was a new mission church. The gravel roads to the church were dusty and noisy. Rocks would fly. I decided the streets should be paved. We had about twelve blocks that led to the church one way and about four blocks the other. Most of the people who lived in the community were elderly. Signatures from the residents could get the job done by local authorities.

I said, "Father, I believe we can do it." Everybody told me I was out of my mind. After a while I *was* out of my mind trying to get everybody to sign the papers, driving hundreds of miles to find in-laws and out-laws and kinsmen to sign. It took about four or five months, but finally everybody living in the area signed. Then, after all the work was done, the people in the church and in the community were thrilled. It was really a big thing.

The construction crew supervisor who did the paving job was a big, tall man named Gus. He was very likable. His wife would take him lunch, and my mother would send some fruit for the crew.

Finally, when the job was done, I wrote Gus a long letter of appreciation and told him what a fine job he and his crew had done and how much I appreciated it. I had not met Gus. A few days later, Gus's wife stopped me in town. She yelled, "Oscar, come here."

She stood there a moment as big tears welled up in her eyes and said, "You know, Gus has been working for the city for years, and no one has ever written him a letter of appreciation." She continued, "Gus sat down the other night and read your letter over and over and just cried."

The next Sunday Gus and his wife were in church for the first time. Six weeks later, I baptized both of them. Several months later, Gus died of a heart attack.

A letter of appreciation saying you care is another way to build bridges. Write letters of appreciation.

Building bridges takes time, but I do not know of anything if consistently done over the years that will bear more fruit. Several of my students have come back after seminary and said, "This is one of the most fantastic ways to reach people you have not really known very well." Learn about people's times of joy and rejoice with them. Show your interest. That is a start to building bridges.

BUILDING BRIDGES DURING TIMES OF STRESS

SICKNESS

People have many times of stress in their lives, which provide excellent opportunities to build bridges. You may think that people are unreachable during times of sickness; but in the hospital, perhaps in a critical condition, people are open. If you want an opportunity to build bridges, visit people in the hospital. You may even meet Person X there and bring him into your circles.

If you are ever depressed and feeling sorry for yourself, go reach out to people in the hospital. They are hurting, and they need help.

Before you begin to make hospital visits, you need to learn how to visit sick people. So make an appointment with your pastor or another church staff member or ask someone who knows for the name of a book on how to visit people in the hospital. There are some definite dos and don'ts for visiting people in the hospital. These are only a few things to know before visiting a patient, but they are important:

- Don't tell a sick person how bad he looks.
- Don't ask personal or embarrassing questions about the person's condition. If the person doesn't tell you, don't ask.
- Don't tell him about someone with the same condition unless that person is doing well.
- Don't tell him how sorry you feel for him.
- Don't tell him about your own problems.
- Don't share with him all the bad news you have heard.
- Don't sit on the bed.
- Don't stay too long.
- Do go in with a smile on your face and victory in your heart.
- Do share encouraging things.
- Do tell some good things you know that the hospitalized person would be interested in.
- Do stay only a short while.
- Do volunteer to pray for the person.

TIMES OF SORROW OR DEATH

When you reach out and love people during times of sorrow, you have a tremendous opportunity to build relationship bridges. Sometimes we do not know what to say when someone loses a loved one. Remember, your care, concern, and love at this time are far more important than what you say. Sometimes you do not need to say anything. Just being there will make a significant and perhaps lasting impression.

Something that can be very helpful to those who are grieving is to ask them to tell you some of their favorite memories of the loved one who has died. Allowing a person to remember and describe the good memories can provide a great relief to a grieving person. Ask the spouse about how they first met, fell in love, and got married. Ask about favorite holiday experiences and funny experiences they shared together.

A number of little booklets have been written that are very helpful to people who are grieving a loss. One such book is called *Good Grief* by Granger Westburg. He describes ten stages of grief most people can identify with as they go through a grieving process. Giving a copy of such a book to a person during a time of loss may be a great blessing and a very practical help. Give the book as a gift with a personal note inside. That way the person doesn't have to worry about returning it. He may even want to share it with other family members who are grieving.

Remember to be attentive two or three or four weeks after a loss. Sometimes that is when the pressure really hits because it is the decision-making time. A good listener is often needed at this time. Send prayer notes, make occasional phone calls, drop by for a visit, or take the person out to lunch or dinner. Just providing an opportunity to talk about the loss can be very healing.

Put the date on your calendar for next year and contact the person on the anniversary of the loss. That is another time when a grieving person needs some comfort. You may also want to make a contact during the first year when special holidays roll around. Those are times when memories are strong and grief may be difficult to handle. A friend who remembers at such times means much to a grieving person.

OTHER TIMES OF STRESS

If you can reach out and build bridges to people in times of stress, they will never forget you. Other opportunities to build relationship bridges are times of:
- a financial reversal,
- the loss of a job,
- a crisis in marriage,
- a crisis with children.

As you pray for those in your concentric circles, watch for and seek out times to build relationship bridges. Keep your eyes and ears open to opportunities that may arise. Trust that God will call them to your attention also. After all, he is more interested in reaching people than you are. This is the key: building relationship bridges through our concentric circles.

I tell my students that if they are not continually bumping into people who have needs, they had better be concerned because it may mean that God has not counted them worthy to be a channel of his love. Of course, a person's deepest need is Christ. As you build bridges, opportunities will open for you to share the gospel.

PERSONALIZING CHAPTER 13

Using a journal or notebook, respond to the following questions or activities. Record details that will help you understand and apply the truths of this chapter to your own life.

1. What are some ways you have experienced the relationship bridge building of others? What did they do that was most meaningful or helpful? How did their actions affect your attitudes or feelings toward them?

2. What are some of the ways you have built relationship bridges in the past? Were these actions related to times of joy, stress, or other circumstances?

3. Have you ever "blown it" in building relationship bridges? How? What could you have done differently to have a positive effect?

4. As you pray through your survey, ask the Lord to reveal ways you can build relationship bridges with the people for whom you are praying. Write notes on your survey sheets as God gives you ideas or insights on how to reach out to particular people. Pray especially for those on your "Most Wanted" list.

5. Before you get together with your small group, try to do at least one thing this week that will contribute to building a relationship bridge.

BUILDING UP THE BODY

Use the following questions and activities with your small group to help one another apply these truths to your lives and to build up the body of Christ.

1. Share with one another meaningful experiences you have had that resulted from the bridge-building activity of someone else. Describe your feelings about the experience and your attitude toward the person.

146

2. What are some of the ways you have built relationship bridges in the past?

3. What are some times or ways you have "blown it" in building relationship bridges, and how do you think you could have done things differently to have a positive effect?

4. Based upon the people you already have listed in your survey, what are some ways you sense God may want you to build relationship bridges and with whom?

5. Discuss ways that your group working together might have the opportunity to build relationship bridges with an individual, a family, or a group. Perhaps your group can become a spiritual SWAT team.

6. Spend some time together in prayer for one another and for the people you sense God is leading you to build relationship bridges with. Ask the Lord to reveal ways of building bridges to these individuals, families, or groups.

7. What have you done or experienced in the past week as a result of our study thus far? How is God working in your relationships?

8. Ask each small-group member: *How can we pray for you this week?* Then take time to pray for these specific needs or requests.

Stage 5

Show Love:
Show God's Love
by Meeting Needs

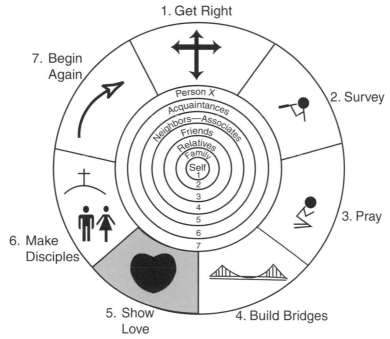

1. Get Right

7. Begin Again

2. Survey

3. Pray

4. Build Bridges

5. Show Love

6. Make Disciples

Person X
Acquaintances
Neighbors—Associates
Friends
Relatives
Family
Self
1
2
3
4
5
6
7

STAGE 5 SUMMARY

SHOW GOD'S LOVE BY MEETING NEEDS

One of the best ways to be used by God in reaching your world is by showing God's love. Love is meeting needs. As God engineers circumstances in the lives of those for whom you are praying, he will create opportunities for these people to experience his love through your life. As he loves people through you by meeting their needs, he will begin drawing these people to his Son.

God engineers the circumstances for love to be shown. God works in your heart to motivate you to love people who may not be very lovely. God also provides the resources to meet needs through you. Your life becomes a channel of God's love.

When you allow God's love to flow through you, people will experience God. They will know they have been loved by a heavenly Father. They will begin to sense his invitation to become a part of his family by adoption and by the saving grace of his Son.

Chapter Fourteen

SHOW GOD'S LOVE BY MEETING NEEDS

One day as I talked to the class about reacting to circumstances, I said, "God will place you in circumstances in which he wants to love someone through you. If you do not react in agape love—depending on the Holy Spirit, abiding in the Word, trusting in him—you are going to blow it."

After class, Jerry came to me and said, "Dr. Thompson, your class is about to plow me under."

I asked, "What's the matter, Jerry?"

He said, "Well, you were talking to me [he personalized it] about God's drawing people into my concentric circles. You said he engineers circumstances to bring people into my life and how I respond either gives me the opportunity to share the gospel with them or lose it."

"That's right," I replied.

He said, "I think I blew it."

I said, "Tell me about it."

So Jerry told me this story. "I work in Dallas and drive my motorbike to work each day. For the last two days, as I have pulled into the parking lot, I have noticed a bike exactly like mine; only it does not have a mirror.

"When I came out to the parking lot last night, my mirror was missing. So I walked down to the other bike, and there it was. My mirror was on his bike. I knew it was my mirror because it was marked.

"I took my mirror off his bike and was so very angry that I flooded his bike. It did not hurt his bike, but it probably took about thirty minutes for him to start it. When I got home, the Lord really began to deal with me. What do I do?"

"Well, I am not sure, Jerry," I said. "What is the Holy Spirit telling you to do?"

Jerry turned and went off muttering, "That is what I thought you would say."

That was Friday. Jerry came back to class the next week and said, "May I share something with the class?

"Friday night I went back to work, and there was this fellow's bike. I said to myself, *I need to treat this fellow as if he were a dear friend and he has a need. Apparently his need is a mirror because he had stolen mine.* I went to the store and bought a mirror just like mine and put it on his bike. I also left a note. I said, 'I know you stole my mirror. I am the one who flooded your bike. But because of a relationship I have with Jesus Christ, he would not tolerate that attitude in my life.' I left the mirror and note with my name and phone number on it.

"That next night the fellow called me. He said, 'I have stolen many things in my life, but I have never received this kind of reaction. Can we talk?'

"That night in my apartment, that guy got down on his knees and gave his life to Jesus."

God leads us, as he did Jerry, into circumstances. He leads you into circumstances with your family, your neighbors, the people at work, and everywhere you go, so that he can reveal himself through you.

LOVING GOD

God designed human beings for love. From the Genesis to the Revelation, we are given one command from the Father over and over again—LOVE.

In Deuteronomy 6:5, we read, "You shall love the Lord your God with all your heart and with all your soul and with all your might."

In the New Testament, we are told that the first and greatest commandment is to love God with all our hearts and souls and minds (see Matt. 22:37–38; Mark 12:30).

You might ask, "How do I love God?"

One morning, after a class in which we had discussed the concept that love is meeting needs, one of my students, Rob, was walking down the hall to the elevator with me.

Rob said, "Dr. Thompson, I am not really sure I understand something. I understand what you are saying about love is meeting needs and that God wants to meet even the deepest need of people through me. But the first and great commandment is to love the Lord God with all our hearts, souls, and minds. The Bible says to love the Lord first, but Dr.

Thompson, how do I love God? He doesn't have any needs. How am I going to show God that I love him?"

And I said, "My dear friend, Matthew 25:35–40 gives us the answer to that question. In this Scripture passage, Jesus said, 'I was hungry, and you gave Me something to eat; I was thirsty, and you gave Me drink; I was a stranger, and you invited Me in; naked, and you clothed Me; I was sick, and you visited Me; I was in prison, and you came to Me.' And then Jesus said, 'to the extent that you did it to one of these brothers of Mine, even the least of them, you did it to Me.'"

When you love people in Jesus' name, you are loving Jesus. When those who are precious to Jesus become precious to you, you are loving God with all of your heart and soul and mind. You are not really loving Jesus until you become a channel of his love in meeting others' needs. Love is meeting needs.

In Matthew 22:39 and Mark 12:31, we find that the second great commandment is, "You shall love your neighbor as yourself."

LOVING OTHERS

When Jesus becomes Lord of your life, you forfeit forever the right to choose whom you will love. You may say, "I just love the world." All right, do you love Bill?

"No," you say, "he is cantankerous. I don't love him."

Then what about Sue?

"Well, I love almost everybody but Sue."

The reason God leaves you in this clay house as long as he does is so that he can reach down to you and through you and reveal himself to a world. That is the reason you occupy space and take up oxygen. He wants to love through you. Love is meeting needs.

THE REVELATION OF LOVE

"For God so loved the world, that he gave his only begotten Son, that whosoever believeth in him should not perish, but have everlasting life" (John 3:16, KJV). God loved us, and he met our needs.

"God demonstrates His own love toward us, in that while we were yet sinners, Christ died for us" (Rom. 5:8). Love is meeting needs. God wants to meet your needs, and he wants to meet the needs of others through you.

There are three Greek words that are translated "love." The first is *eros*. It is the sexual, passionate, fleshly love. There is nothing wrong with it. God designed it for you within the confines of marriage.

The second is the word *philia*. This is a love in which the quality of relationship is stressed. Are there some people you just like to be around? That is *philia*. It is a good love. It is a Christian love. It is a love of feeling, of emotion. It is good when you can say, "I not only love my wife, but I like her too." This is the word we are talking about.

The third word for love in Scripture is *agape*. It is not necessarily based on feeling. It is pure, reasoned, logical volition. It is a love based on a choice you make. It is a God-like love that is unconditional.

Sometimes we have to see the love of God, the white heat of the love of God, over against the literal holiness of God. God's love needs to be seen against his holiness.

When the great revival came in 1734 to Northampton, Massachusetts, Jonathan Edwards had preached a series of sermons entitled, "The Justice of God in the Damnation of Sinners." People saw for the first time the holiness of God. That was when revival came.

God is a holy God. Genuine revival will never come in our land and we will never learn the great love of God until it is seen against his glorious holiness. He demands holy living from his people.

Agape is a sacred love. What do I mean by sacred love? Well, remember Esau? The Scriptures say that Esau was a profane man. That does not necessarily mean he was a "cusser." He probably was, but that is not what profane means in this context. It means that nothing was sacred in Esau's life. In other words, everything had a price. His birthright, which should have been the most precious thing in his life, had a price.

We look at our secular society today. Everything has a price. Does your word have a price? My dad said to me, "Son, your word is your bond. I do not care what it costs you. Tell the truth. Your word must be sacred. It does not have a price."

If love is not sacred, when you distill it to its final essence, then it has a price. God's love does not have a price. It is pure. It will go to all lengths. It does not call for payment. It is sacred. It is holy.

God's love is unconditional and freely given. It is sacred and needs to flow through a clean and holy channel. You can show God's love for others by choosing to meet their needs. *Agape* means: *here is a need; I am going to meet that need.*

You say, "But I must feel something for people before I love them."

THE REASON FOR LOVE

Let me ask you this. What kind of feeling did Jesus have when he died on the cross for us? It was not a feeling that sent him to the cross, dear friend. It was our need that sent him to the cross. He had a deep feeling for us, but the feeling came because he looked at our sin and he saw our deep need. That *agape* love transcended the agony of the cross. By his act, he said, "I will meet your needs." He saw our need and met it.

Now do not tell me about winning the world if you cannot love your neighbor. Do not tell me about winning the world if you do not take time to meet the needs of your own child or spouse. You are to be a channel of love. Start in your "Jerusalem." Start in your home.

Agape is meeting needs. I was a pastor for about twenty years. Often at about 5:30 in the afternoon, I just did not get very excited about going visiting that evening. Have you ever felt that way? When those times come, what do we do? We say, "Lord Jesus, I love you, and I am going visiting because I love you." It is an *agape* love.

Love Is . . .
NOT a word of emotion,
NOT a word of feeling.
Rather, love is
A word of reason,
A word of volition or will,
A word of action.
Love is doing!
Love builds relationships;
Love maintains relationships;
Love fulfills relationships;
Love initiates relationships.
Love is meeting needs!

HOW DO WE LOVE PEOPLE?

So we ask, "How do we love people?" We are to love people the same way God loves people—by meeting their needs.

"You have heard that it was said, 'YOU SHALL LOVE YOUR NEIGHBOR, and hate your enemy.' But I say to you, love your enemies, and pray for those who persecute you" (Matt. 5:43–44).

How do you love your enemies? What does God say? Find someone you love, and treat your enemy the very same way you treat the one you love. Love is treating all people the very same way. When Jesus becomes

Lord of your life, you forfeit forever the right to choose whom you will love.

James 2:8–9 says that if you really keep the royal law found in Scripture, "You shall love your neighbor as yourself," you are doing right. But if you show favoritism, you sin and are convicted by the law as law-breakers.

I am going to tell you a story from Matthew 5:45. Let us reverently pretend for a moment that you are the Lord. You have two fellows down here on earth who are both farmers. One of those farmers honors you. He says, "Lord, I love You." He gives of the increase of his ground, and he bows down and worships you.

But the other farmer across the fence disrespects you, takes your name in vain, does not give any of the increase back to you, and in every way abhors you.

Now if you were God—here comes our reaction—what would you do? You would give rain and sunshine to the fellow who loves you. Right? You would turn the other fellow's water off. Isn't that right? That is our natural reaction. But what did Jesus say? "He causes his sun to rise on the evil and on the good, and sends rain on the righteous and on the unright-eous."

You are going to find all kinds of people who are not lovely in your concentric circles. You work with them at the office, and they are just as cantankerous as they can be. They are not receptive to you, but you begin to pray: "Father, reveal to me their needs. Here I am. You know all the responsibilities I have, but wherever I go and whomever my life touches, I will be salt. I will be salt to touch and preserve, to help and heal and love."

When you find that person out there who is just impossible, you say, "Father, engineer circumstances in his life to draw him to you, to meet his need."

So we see that the genuine, God-given *agape* love does not depend on a feeling. Feelings fluctuate; love is stable. Love stems from a deep motivation that does not come from circumstances. That motivation must come totally disconnected from circumstances or it will not be profitable.

Genuine love does not depend on the person whom you are loving to return that love or to be receptive to that love or to love first.

GOD LEADS US INTO CIRCUMSTANCES

Now I realize that what I am suggesting is not practical in today's world, but it works because it is God who works through you! Let me ask you this, Who else is going to love like this? Jesus said, "Whoever shall force you to go one mile, go with him two" (Matt. 5:41).

Here again I have a very fertile imagination. I look out into a field and see a Jewish boy doing some pruning in the vineyard. It was a Roman law in those days that the soldiers could ask the Jews to carry their baggage for one mile.

A Roman soldier comes along and says, "Boy, come here. I want you to carry my baggage."

The infuriated Jewish boy, with white knuckles and clenched teeth, climbs over the fence. As he climbs over, he knocks some rocks off the fence, which angers him even more. If looks could kill! Well, he picks up the baggage but does not say a thing. When he comes to the end of that mile, he drops that baggage like a hot rock, turns on his heels, and returns to his work in the vineyard.

The next day the Roman soldier passes by that same vineyard. He looks out and sees someone he thinks is the same boy and decides to aggravate him again.

The Roman soldier says, "Boy, come and carry my baggage again."

The boy looks up and says, "Good morning, sir," bolts the fence, picks up the baggage, and says, "What is your destination?"

The Roman soldier says, "I am going to Caesarea. I am going back to Rome."

"Do you have a family?" the boy asks.

"Yes," says the Roman soldier. "A wife and three children."

The boy involves the Roman in conversation. They come to the end of the first mile. The Roman sees it; the Jewish boy ignores it.

Finally, the boy and the Roman soldier come to the end of the second mile. The boy says, "Well, I must get back to my work."

The Roman says, "Son, didn't you see the mile marker back there? You went two miles."

"Oh," the boy says, "I know. But my master says, 'Whoever shall force you to go one mile, go with him two.'"

But you say, "That is going to cost me."

I ask you, "Did it cost Jesus to go to the cross?"

Remember, love is action. It is doing. Love is meeting needs. Our attitude is formed on the immediacy of who is in control—Jesus or me? I form an attitude, and out of that attitude, I react.

There is only one way we can be what Jesus wants us to be. We must not agree with the old sinful selfish nature. We must agree with Christ and do things his way. That is submission to the authority of the King.

157

When that happens, he is glorified, and people see Jesus in me. Agreeing with Jesus is not natural. It is supernatural.

Many of our opportunities to share the Lord are blocked and the Spirit of God is quenched because we react wrongly to circumstances. We react as the world reacts, and that just does not work in pointing people to the Lord.

You may ask, "What kind of love is this *agape* love?"

The Bible says, "Owe nothing to anyone except to love one another; for he who loves his neighbor has fulfilled the law" (Rom. 13:8). Go right down the Ten Commandments. You are not going to steal from someone you really love. You are not going to kill someone you love. Neither would you commit adultery against someone you love.

GOD PROVIDES THE RESOURCES FOR MEETING NEEDS

God's plan for your life is that his love flow through your life and reach out to others and meet their needs. You do not meet their needs out of your reservoir. You meet needs out of God's reservoir. Isn't that great?

"Father, I want to be a channel. The reason you leave me in this clay house, in this body, as long as you do is to flow through me and reach out and take hold of people and build a relationship to them, a relationship cemented by *agape* love."

So I develop a relationship with anyone, and God draws that person to himself through that relationship. So we have our concentric circles. We have our relationships. We show God's love through those relationships by meeting needs, and people come to see and know God through us.

GOD PROVIDES THE MOTIVATION FOR LOVE

Some people in our concentric circles may not be lovable. You may say, "I cannot love that person." But remember, God loves him. If we are going to be in agreement with God, then we must love the one whom God loves and meet his needs.

You do not get your motivation for telling the world about Jesus from a love for people. You get your motivation from your love for Jesus. The most important encounter Jesus had with the apostle Peter after the resurrection was at the morning seaside breakfast.

"Peter, do you love me? Feed my sheep."

Peter could have replied, "Lord, I do not love sheep. I am a fisherman."

And the Lord could have said, "Peter, I did not ask if you loved sheep. I asked if you loved me" (see John 21:15–17).

Seeing the needs of humanity will never be enough motivation to love the world. There are many altruistic people who go out to meet the needs of the world by giving out of their own resources until they are drained dry. Their resources are not adequate. So their idealism turns to disillusionment. Often the disillusionment turns to bitterness, and the bitterness causes broken relationships. A case in point is the altruistic preacher who gives and gives until his own well runs dry. His motive is to meet others' needs so that he may have his own needs met.

Others sense his real motive and turn from it. The preacher leaves the ministry, disturbed and empty, feeling frustration and failure.

You Are the Channel for God's Love

Little does this frustrated person realize that he is not the source to meet others' needs, but only the channel. A person needs to realize that his resources and his love are from God, and he must draw them from him. Otherwise, a person practices a humanism that cannot stand up under the demands of today's world.

Our love for God must precede our love for the lost. If we love God, we will love the one whom God loves. To love without action, without meeting needs, is not love. Every time you find God loving man, God is meeting needs.

When you look out through your concentric circles, you will say: "Father, here I am. I go to your great reservoir of love, and I depend upon that great funnel of your love to flow through me to meet the needs of those around me."

If you would begin to meet the needs of those in your family, you would get your own needs met. Sometimes we say, "No one loves me, and no one is meeting my needs. Why should I meet anybody else's?"

Well, I will tell you. It is the genius of the gospel. You go to the cross and die to self. Every Christian needs to work through Romans 6 and 7. You are to die to self and then let Jesus become alive in you. Then he funnels his love through you.

Personalizing Chapter 14

Using a journal or notebook, respond to the following questions or activities. Record details that will help you understand and apply the truths of this chapter to your own life.

1. Think about Jerry's story of the motorcycle mirror at the beginning of the chapter. Have you "blown it" with someone in one of your circles because of a bad attitude, a wrong response, or an offensive action? Do you lack a clear conscience because of what that person knows about you? If so, think about what you might need to say or write to that person. You might even use Jerry's words:

   "I . . . [what you have done that was wrong] . . . But because of a relationship I have with Jesus Christ, he would not tolerate that attitude [action, or behavior] in my life."

   Work on getting the relationship right first. Get a clear conscience. Then think about that person's needs. Begin to intercede for him or her. Ask the Lord to reveal a need you can meet to demonstrate love.

2. As you are praying through your survey, ask God to identify, reveal, or make you aware of the needs of the people you are praying for. Show his love by meeting the needs of your family. Show his love by meeting a need in the life of one of the persons on your "Most Wanted" list.

BUILDING UP THE BODY

Use the following questions and activities with your small group to help one another apply these truths to your lives and to build up the body of Christ.

1. Describe specific instances in which you have experienced God's love through others who met your needs. What did they do? How did you respond?

2. What are some ways God is teaching you to show love by meeting needs of others?

3. Are there ways you are struggling with the idea of meeting needs? Discuss your feelings and attitudes. Help each other consider ways of overcoming these difficulties. Take these matters to the Lord and pray for the individuals and the situations with which they are struggling.

4. Stop to consider the individuals in your small group. Do any of them have needs that God wants to meet through you or through the group? You may even want to ask the question, *Are there ways that you would allow us to show God's love to you by meeting a special need you have?* If the needs that surface are beyond the means of

your group, begin praying for the way God will provide for those needs.

5. What have you done or experienced in the past week as a result of our study thus far? How is God working in your relationships?

6. Ask each small-group member: *How can we pray for you this week?* Then take time to pray for these specific needs or requests.

Chapter Fifteen

*L*OVING IN *C*ONCENTRIC *C*IRCLES

MEETING THE FAMILY'S NEEDS

Let me tell you how I try to meet my family's needs every day. First I ask myself, what is my daily responsibility to my wife Carolyn? God has put me into her life, and I accept his conditions for my relationship to her. I am here to meet her needs, whatever those needs may be.

Then I have a daughter Damaris. She is fourteen years old, blond, green-eyed, and irrepressible. She just keeps coming.

Damaris has a dog named Neigette, which in French means "snowflake." He is white and very "flaky." When the alarm goes off in the morning, I cringe. Damaris opens her bedroom door and here comes Neigette. Our bedroom is about seventeen feet long. Neigette takes about three steps, flies through the air, and lands on me. Then I get my unwanted morning bath.

I yell for Damaris to get the dog. She replies, "He is just loving you." I do not have that kind of need!

Damaris has learned a lot from hearing me speak. She has learned the language. I always know if she really has a need, because when she does, she sits down and very maturely explains what the need is.

Sometimes she just comes popping through and says, "I have a need," and keeps going. It is like going through and dropping a fifty-cent piece in the proverbial slot machine and pulling the lever. Who knows? Dad might be in the right mood, and she might hit the jackpot. So that is Damaris.

Then there is my dear eighty-two-year-old mother. She loves everything in sight. What a precious soul she is. She has a ministry of writing. I suppose she writes close to one hundred letters a month. She does not just write empty, sentimental little notes. She writes sweet notes that meet needs and also uplift and encourage people.

One day I said to her, "Dear, how do you do it?"

"Well," she replied, "Honey, when I miss Oscar [my father], when I get lonely, when I get afraid, or when I become blue missing Oscar's touch or his voice, I find somebody who has a need. I allow the Lord to reach out to that person through me. When I comfort others, God comforts me."

These three people are my Immediate Family, my Circle 2. "But," you may say, "your second circle does not have any lost people in it." That's right. But if you are not loving those in your Circle 2, you are surely not going to love those in your Circle 7 very well. You see, this lifestyle is one of loving the saved and the lost. My Circle 2 is a place for me to practice loving others by meeting their needs. It's a place for me to help my family learn to show love by meeting needs in their concentric circles too.

Now back to Carolyn, whom I list on a survey sheet all by herself. I love Carolyn, so when I begin to pray for her, I say, "Father, what are her needs?" Love is meeting needs.

One of my friends said, "You know, I really did not know what my wife's needs were until I asked her. One of her needs is to get out of the house occasionally and go shopping. She likes me to go with her, but I do not really like to go. That is one of her needs, so I go anyway."

I understand how my friend feels. I grew up with a mother and two older sisters who loved to go shopping. Since I was the baby brother, I had to go along.

"Be quiet. Stand still. We will be through in a little while," they would say. A little while could mean anywhere from five minutes to six hours. It usually meant the latter.

Well, my wife is just like my mother and two sisters. When we go to the mall, we walk from one end to the other at least six times. We shop at every shop. We look at everything in each shop, and I do believe that we almost always go back to that first shop and buy the first thing she saw.

Though I detest shopping, I do it because Carolyn likes for me to go along with her. I have learned that whatever her needs are, whatever it costs, that is what I want to do to love her.

A CHRISTIAN MARRIAGE

In our day and time, the trouble is that we do not understand what Jesus meant when he spoke of love. We usually base marriage on the idea that "I love me and I want you to make me happy. If you do not make me happy, then I am going to split."

That is not a Christian marriage. A Christian marriage means I am committing myself first to Jesus Christ and then to my wife. Because my commitment is first to Christ, I accept my wife on his conditions with all the immeasurable love that he has. My attitude toward her is going to be like Jesus' attitude toward the church. He loved it, and he poured out his life for it.

If you are not yet married, do not settle for anything less. I am absolutely serious. That is the relationship I have with my dear, beautiful, glorious, wonderful wife.

Teaching Your Family about Relationships

I am already trying to teach this principle of love to my daughter. Damaris came in the other morning and stuck her head into the dressing room. "Daddy, Western Day is at school today."

"That's great. So?" I answered.

"May I wear your hat?"

My first reaction was, "Of course not!" My hat was a fifty-dollar gift. It is a beautiful, straw hat I enjoy wearing sometimes in the summer. Besides, it was raining that morning. Damaris is just at that age when all the boys would want to knock her hat off. I know! I used to do that myself. Guess what? She wore my fifty-dollar hat! But her mother wrapped it in cellophane. Carolyn knew how to meet Damaris's need and mine. Love is meeting needs.

Many people are not learning that love is meeting needs at home. Our best school for teaching relationships—the home—is not teaching as it should be. We have tried to place the task elsewhere: schools, church, Sunday school, youth organizations, and government. But the home is where we need to learn to be what we are.

A Homesick Wife

I shared this principle in class one day. Several days later, one of my students came to my office and said, "Dr. Thompson, I really blew it."

I said, "Oh! Tell me about it."

He said, "We have just started seminary, and my wife has been homesick. This is the first time she has ever lived a long distance from her family. The house we have here is so much less than the one we left. Anyway, yesterday she was just miserable. She said she didn't know what to do. I know God wants us here. I began to lecture her. I said, 'Honey, you know that God has called us here. You know that this is our calling'."

His lecture was such a "blessing" to her. She became quiet and defeated. He felt so pious as he went off to study Greek. That's one reason I tell my students, "Preach to the congregations, not to your wives!"

The next morning in class, God captured that student. The man said, "I did not meet that woman's needs." He went back to her and asked, "Honey, forgive me? I am so blind that I do not even know what your needs are."

She said, "I was just lonely, afraid, and insecure in a new city, in a new life. I love you. All I wanted was for you to put your arms around me and hold me and say, 'Baby, it is all right!'"

Do you see where we are going? Has this ever happened to you? Are there times when you need to take your child in your arms and just listen? Are there times when you need to turn the "box" off and listen to your family? Learn their needs, and then meet their needs.

A HUSBAND'S NEEDS

Several months ago, I was teaching a night session for our seminary students' wives. We were talking about concentric circles.

After our second meeting, one of the wives asked to talk with me. She said, "My husband has been discouraged with one of his classes. I work all day long. I arrive at home after a hard day's work and rush to get dinner. Then I walk to our session. He could at least bring me. But after the evening session last week, as I got to the door of our house, I had that ringing in my ears, 'Love is meeting needs! Love is meeting needs!'"

She continued, "The first thing I saw when I walked through the door was my husband sitting in his easy chair watching the football game."

He said, "Honey, will you bathe the kids and put them to bed?"

She said, "There were the dirty dishes from dinner. The house was a wreck. He had done nothing all day long." She sighed and continued, "I took a deep breath. I did not feel very loving, but I decided to trust the Lord to love through me. What are his needs? Well, the first is for me not to create a scene." So she said to her husband, "I have been wanting to see the children all day. This will give me an opportunity to be with them."

By the time she had changed clothes and started to get the children, she heard the bath water running. He had already begun to bathe the children.

He said, "If you will towel off this one, I will take care of the other one."

She continued, "You know, God began to do something in my heart toward my husband. There has been so much pressure between us lately.

It all seems to be gone. I have come to realize that my own responsibility before God is to be his channel for meeting needs."

A word of warning: I want to discuss with you something very important about relationships at this point. Husbands and wives, read this very carefully. Underline it! Remember it!

When you accept Jesus Christ's conditions for marriage,

it means that no other human

is to be closer to you than your mate.

If you let a close friend or relative be closer than your mate, something is radically wrong with your relationship. That is the reason a child leaves father and mother. Until marriage, that is the closest relationship. Marriage changes the parent-child relationship. Sometimes people do not realize this. But it is extremely important in the marriage relationship.

MEETING CHILDREN'S NEEDS

Now, what about the children? What about their needs? You see, God has put us in a school—the home. The subject is relationships. Parents are to meet children's needs. Babies cannot meet their own needs. Parents have to. If you really want to meet your children's needs, you will train them to love other children and to meet their needs.

Something really thrills me. Damaris, as I said, is fourteen. She is the joy of my life. There is always something new with her. She seems to make more money than I do. I kid you not. The other day, we were at the restaurant, and I said, "Oh, Honey, I am fresh out." She said, "Daddy, I will take care of it." She whipped out a ten-dollar bill and paid for our lunch. She is a baby-sitter. At our church we have a program where teens are taught to take care of children. The Red Cross, the fire fighters, and police officers all come in and teach them what to do in case of emergencies.

Damaris is a licensed baby-sitter. The kids all over the hill where we live love her. She gets more calls now than I do. When she gets calls, she puts them down in her little calendar date book; then off she goes to baby-sit. Sometimes she doesn't get home until 1:00 or 1:30 A.M., but I always wait up for her.

Damaris loves the children. I know that my little girl is growing up because she is learning to love. She is learning to meet needs. It is beautiful.

When I pray for Damaris, I relate to my daughter's needs. I ask myself, *Who are the people who will have an influence on her?* Obviously, her teachers. I list all of her teachers on Damaris's survey sheet, and I pray for them.

You had better pray for the people who have authority over your children. They will influence them.

LISTEN TO MEET NEEDS

Fathers and mothers, we need to listen to our children. We need to listen to our teens and hear from them what their needs are. Sometimes what we feel their needs to be are not really what they are at all. Listen. Teens are crying out for love, crying out for mothers and fathers to really know what they are going through and to really know what their needs are.

A seventeen-year-old bounced into my office one day. She seemed to be a little rebel on wheels. But she broke down and cried as she admitted, "If only my parents would tell me one time when to get in at night! Do they really care?"

Parents, we do not need to drive our children away from us. We need to be praying for these children whom God has given us. We need to be praying for the Holy Spirit to speak to them, to convict them. But most important—and please do not miss this—we need to be praying for the Holy Spirit to make us the kind of mothers and fathers our children need. We must pray that we will listen, that we will hear, that we will meet their needs. There is no better success story in the world than that of a mother and father who can look at their child who has developed into a man or woman who radiates the character of Jesus Christ, who knows and cares about the needs of others. Friends, that is success!

A LOST SON

I had a student last year who asked us to pray with him about his thirteen-year-old son. He was beginning to be rebellious and had not come to know the Lord. We began to pray for him, but we also prayed for that daddy to be the kind of father his son needed.

About three months later, the fellow came into class and said, "I have something to say. Last night my son ran into my bedroom in the middle of the night and cried out, 'Daddy, I'm lost.'"

Of course, spiritual dad that he was, he said, "Son, you're not lost. You're right here in the house with Mother and Dad."

His son cried, "No, Daddy, I am lost. I am lost from God! I am lost from the Lord!" Daddy finally caught on, got up, and shared the gospel. His son trusted the Lord. The boy was not convinced by his dad, but he was convicted by the Holy Spirit in answer to prayer. That is why we have a focus on intercessory prayer.

LOVING THE ONE WHO BUGS YOU

As you meet others' needs, you receive a wonderful by-product. When you love other people, God gives dividends. You receive love from God and others.

Years ago when I was pastoring, a teenage girl came blasting into my office one evening. She was a redheaded, vivacious, never-hit-the-ground type of personality. She came charging in, plunked down in a chair, cried a few crocodile tears, and sobbed, "Brother Oscar, I am so unhappy."

"Tell me about it," I answered

She replied, "Nobody loves me."

Do you know what my pastoral response was? You will think this is so professorial and so dignified. I said, "Good grief, Brenda. I know your parents. I know they are busy with their new business, but they love you. I know your friends. They love you."

"No, they don't," she replied. "Nobody loves me. I could just die, and nobody cares."

I said, "Brenda, let me ask you a question. Are you a Christian?" She looked shocked and said, "Brother Oscar, you know I am a Christian."

I said, "Brenda, who told you someone was supposed to love you anyway!"

"What do you mean?" she asked.

I said, "In the economy of God, you have been created by him as a channel for love to flow through you to others. The trouble is that you want the flow to go the wrong way. That is the reason you are miserable. When the flow of love is going the right way, as you were designed, you will not feel this way. You are supposed to do the loving. The person who always has to have the stream of love flowing inward is going to become a stagnant pool. Brenda, I believe you are stagnant.

"You go find some people out there and meet their needs. You do not have to feel great about them. You do not have to feel good about loving them. You do not have to have any feeling. From the heart, you just make a decision, 'Dear God, whatever people you put in my path, I am going to show your love by meeting their needs.'

"Now," I said, "tomorrow I want you to make yourself available to the Lord Jesus. I want you to get alone with him. In the morning, I want you to love somebody. Who is there out there that would be really difficult for you to love?"

Immediately, she replied, "Judy."

"Who is Judy?" I asked.

"Judy is a freshman," Brenda said. "She is just dumb. She rides the bus with me, and," she continued, "she just bugs me."

I said, "Well, what is the problem?"

Brenda said, "I have to ride with her forty-five minutes every day. She crawls on the bus, and it is chatter, chatter, chatter. I just do not want to listen to that freshman. She just latches on to me. I am a senior."

"Well, out of your immense senior wisdom, why don't you meet some of the needs of this lowly little freshman's ignorance." And we both laughed.

"Assignment number one is for you to love Judy. That is my prescription. Now, I have to go to a meeting. I will see you Sunday." I realize that I was using direct counseling, but it worked.

Well, Brenda came back Sunday, and this was her story. "I got on the bus Thursday morning. No sooner than I sat down, here came Judy. She sat down right beside me. It just really bugged me. I said, 'Lord, I am going to meet her need if it kills me.' The best thing I thought I could do was just listen. So I turned to her, and for the first time, I looked at her while she was talking to me. As I looked at her, I began to see a little face I had never noticed before. I realized that underneath all that chatter was a hurting little girl.

"As we continued to talk, I said, 'Judy, tell me about your brothers and sisters and mom and dad.' She became very still and quiet and was silent for a while. Finally, she said, 'Brenda, my mom and dad are getting a divorce, and I am so scared. We are going to have to move, and my whole world is coming apart.'"

Brenda said, "Brother Oscar, in that moment I just listened. That is all I did, but I felt the love of God wanting to meet that little girl's needs through me. I put my arm around her, and we talked until we arrived at school.

"After getting off the bus, Judy put her books on the ground and put her arms around me and said, 'Oh, Brenda, I just love you.'"

She said, "Brother Oscar, after I had met Judy's need, I went around all day looking for someone else to love. I arrived at home that afternoon and went in the front door. There sat Kim, my little sister, a seventh grader. She was watching 'Popeye.' The house looked like the aftermath of World War III. My little sister bugs me too."

Brenda said she turned to her little sister and said, "Kim, have you seen that program before?"

"Seventeen times," Kim answered.

Brenda asked, "Do you have any homework?"

"Yes, I have algebra, but I do not know how to do it."

"Well," said Brenda, "suppose you spread your homework out on the kitchen table, and I will help you with it."

Brenda said that her little sister looked at her like a calf looks at a new gate and exclaimed, "You are going to help me with my homework?"

"Yes," Brenda replied, "I will be back in a minute."

Kim muttered, "I do not believe this!"

Brenda continued, "I sat down, and Kim and I worked through the algebra. I explained the problems that she did not understand. Then I suggested that we clean her room."

Brenda told me that they cleaned Kim's room and then cleaned the rest of the house. The girls then prepared the evening meal. Their parents usually arrived home around 7:00.

When their parents arrived, the house was clean and a hot meal awaited them on the table. The girls almost had to get the smelling salts to revive them. As the family ate, they relaxed and enjoyed being together.

After eating, Brenda showered, dressed, and left on a date.

"When I came home and had dressed for bed, my mother came into my room and sat on my bed and said, 'Honey, I do not know what changed your attitude today. You have been so helpful to all of us. I cannot let you go to sleep tonight without telling you two things. Your little sister came in tonight before she went to bed and said that she really did love her big sister. You know, your dad and I have been so very busy trying to make our new business a success, but we just wanted you to know we love you too.'"

Brenda sat in my office and cried. She said, "Brother Oscar, all this time it has been *me, my, mine*. I have been trying to get my status in the world and struggling with my peer group. I have learned that when the flow of love is outward, I am meeting the needs of others, and my own needs get met too."

Do you have someone in your concentric circles who "bugs you"? Perhaps this person has a deep problem. Perhaps you need to reach out and be sensitive to the person's need. Who is going to help him if you don't? Let me tell you a story.

THE JOYS OF A PRINCE ALBERT TOBACCO CAN

Years ago, there was a one-room schoolhouse out in the country. Students from the first through the tenth grades were taught there.

A little boy in that one-room school was always into something. He had a Prince Albert tobacco can into which he put all his little treasures.

Those of you who have never enjoyed having a Prince Albert tobacco can have never really lived. You can put all kinds of "worms, snails, and puppy dog tails" in a Prince Albert tobacco can.

At recess one day, the little boy found a bumble bee. He put it into his can, and he was delighted. It was so much fun. He could hear ZZZZZZZZZZZZZZZZ in that can. Then the bell rang, and it was time to go back to work.

The little boy put the can in the hip pocket of his jeans and went to class. He could hear ZZZZZZZZZZZZZZ!

Well, this little boy did not understand the physics of a crimped can in a tight jean hip pocket. As a result, when he sat down, the bee got out of the can. The bee was very disturbed about his close quarters, and when he was able to escape from the can, but not from the close confines of the pocket, he immediately began to register his displeasure at such confinement.

The little boy began to hop around on the back row. That bee was really getting to him, if you know what I mean.

Seeing him hop around on that back row, the teacher demanded, "Johnny, what is the matter with you? Sit still!" But he could not sit still. He just kept jumping around. And she said again, "Johnny, sit still!"

To which Johnny replied, "Teacher, there are things going on back here that you don't know nothing about."

THEY ARE HURTING

Johnny's explanation may not be couched in the best grammar, but I believe you get the picture. When you are reaching out to people who "just bug you," or you get a bad reaction from loved ones or friends, you pray for them. They may have things going on in their lives that you know nothing about. They may be in despair. They need your love, not your striking back at them, not your criticism.

Be sensitive to the needs of those about you. There may be things going on that you do not know anything about, and you may be able to reach in and show God's love for them by meeting their needs.

Do you feel isolated? Do you feel that nobody cares about you, nobody loves you, and you get "the blues"? Let me give you a prescription. Go out in your concentric circles and meet someone else's needs.

Now do not go and comfort someone by telling him about all of your problems. That would be like the two fellows at the Golden Gate Bridge. One fellow was up on the bridge getting ready to jump. The other fellow thought, *I believe I can talk him out of it.* So he walked up on the bridge. After they had talked for about forty-five minutes, both of them jumped!

That is not what I have in mind. God has loved you. Now you go out and love somebody else. I have discovered that the happiest people in the world are those who are channels of God's love. Love is meeting needs.

PRACTICING AT CHURCH

IMPLOSION OR EXPLOSION

You love me; I'll love you. You don't love me; I won't love you. We become a mutual admiration society. Have you ever been in churches that have become mutual admiration societies? People who have needs band together. They find a solitude and a comfort in having their own needs met. Then, instead of becoming an *explosion* when their needs have been met, they become cliquish and have an *implosion.*

Do you know what an implosion is? An implosion explodes within and then just consumes itself and collapses. It is just debris. Have you ever seen that happen in a church? We begin to love one another, and there is no threat. Then we feel threatened when someone new tries to enter our "safe little world." The reason many churches never make it is because they become mutual admiration societies. They "preach the Word" but never reach anybody.

Sunday school classes can become the same way. You see, when we are threatened and not really sure about ourselves, we feel comfortable only with our friends. Consequently, we do not want strangers coming in and monkeying with our security. God's plan for the church was not to stay in Jerusalem. Likewise, it is not just Jerusalem that we are responsible for. What happened to those believers who stayed in Jerusalem for twelve years, not doing what Jesus told them to do? The fire fell! Persecution hit! You may read through the Book of Acts and think the early Christians went everywhere to preach the gospel. Well, they went everywhere for a while. There were some scattered fires, but then they became self-inclusive, the Jews particularly. They imploded instead of exploding. That will happen to you if you do not know God's design for your life.

UNDERSTANDING THE BODY

Ephesians 4, Romans 12, and 1 Corinthians 12 talk about gifts of the body of Christ, the church. The God-given gift of administration enables a person to recognize a situation and have control over it. I do not have the gift of administration. I could not organize my way out of a brown paper bag. But, I do have the gift of mercy. That is my spiritual gift, and I am a pastor/teacher. I know what my gifts are, and I do not apologize for them. I can walk into a room and within thirty minutes can tell you the people who are hurting. Some of you also have the gift of mercy. Others of you have the gift of administration. We are to work as a body under the headship of Christ to draw the world to him. My gift is not your gift. Do not desire my gift. God's sovereignty gives the gift. Do not start asking God for some specific spiritual gift. He knows what he wants to do with you, and he knows where you fit into the body.

Suppose you are a toe and you say, "Lord, I want to be an eye. God, I just have to be an eye. I want the gift of being an eye."

The Lord says, "No, I made you a toe."

"Lord, I want to be an eye."

"OK, you can be an eye, but the only thing you are ever going to see is the inside of a sock."

We need to recognize our spiritual gifts and use them to build up the body of Christ. This brings us back to loving people—meeting their needs. How can we love someone we have never learned to understand? If Jesus dwells in you and in someone else, it is absurd to say you have a personality clash with that person. Many times these so-called clashes come when two people do not understand their spiritual gifts and how they fit into the body of Christ, the church.

In other words, try to look at the other person from God's point of view. Understand how the other person is to function in the body. If you understand that, you will then be able to understand his actions. If you have the gift of mercy and someone else has the gift of prophecy, in order to accept each other, you are going to have to understand how each of you fits in God's plan for the church.

The church is a place you can practice showing love by meeting needs. In fact, Jesus said that one way people will know his disciples is by the way they love one another. When people see a church filled with people who love each other, they will be drawn to such love. As you practice showing your love to other believers, you will be prepared to show love when these needy people come into your acquaintance—when they enter your concentric circles.

PERSONALIZING CHAPTER 15

Using a journal or notebook, respond to the following questions or activities. Record details that will help you understand and apply the truths of this chapter to your own life.

1. How does God want you to love your family? Take time right now to pray for your immediate family. For each person, ask the Lord what his or her needs are. Ask the Lord what he would like to do through you even today to meet each person's needs. Take notes on your survey sheets for each person. As he reveals things, make a "to-do" list. Start meeting needs for God's pleasure.

2. Have you been hurting silently because a family member seems to be overlooking your needs? Ask God how you can begin the flow of reciprocal love, by loving him or her first. Ask the Lord for wisdom to know what to say, if anything, to let your family members know of your need. They may be so busy or self-consumed that they have failed to pick up on your signals. You may need to be like Damaris and say, "I have a need."

3. Do you have people who really "bug" you? Begin praying right now for the number one person who bugs you. Ask God to reveal what his or her needs are—or at least what one of the needs is. How would God want you to love that person by meeting needs? Make your plan and watch for the next opportunity to carry out the plan.

4. Have you recently become aware of some people who are really hurting for some reason? Ask God if this is your invitation to show love by meeting needs.

5. Take some time thanking God for the ways he has met your needs. Thank him for Jesus and his work for you on the cross. Thank God for the ways he has provided for you. "Count your blessings, name them one by one. Count your many blessings, see what God has done."

BUILDING UP THE BODY

Use the following questions and activities with your small group to help one another apply these truths to your lives and to build up the body of Christ.

1. What are some ways God has led you to meet the needs of family members, and how have they responded? Have you experienced love in return in some special way?

2. Discuss how God would want you to respond, even if your love winds up being primarily one-way love. If the love is not being returned, how would God want you to continue loving? Think about the life of Jesus before you decide where to "draw the line." What would Jesus do? What did he do?

3. How have you experienced God guiding you to love a person who really bugs you? What have you done? How did the person respond? What difference has this had on your own attitude toward this person?

4. What have you done or experienced in the past week as a result of our study thus far? How is God working in your relationships?

5. Ask each small-group member: *How can we pray for you this week?* Then take time to pray for these specific needs or requests.

Stage 6

Make Disciples: Make Disciples and Help Them Grow

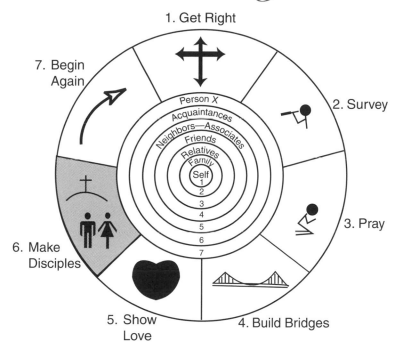

1. Get Right

7. Begin Again

2. Survey

Person X
Acquaintances
Neighbors—Associates
Friends
Relatives
Family
Self
1
2
3
4
5
6
7

3. Pray

6. Make Disciples

4. Build Bridges

5. Show Love

STAGE 6 SUMMARY

MAKE DISCIPLES AND HELP THEM GROW

As you continue to pray, cultivate relationships, and show God's love, you will reach a point where you need to confront people with the claims of Jesus Christ on their lives. When you see other people as God sees them—helplessly lost without Christ, you will want to share with them the good news you know about Christ. You will point them to God and his conditions for salvation.

Your responsibility is to bear witness of the Christ who lives in you, to tell about your faith in him. The Holy Spirit is the one with the responsibility of bringing conviction of sin. He is the one who convinces people of the truth of the gospel. When people yield their lives to Christ, you will be able to rejoice with the angels in heaven. You will experience the joy of being used by God to see a miracle happen in changing a life.

After people turn to Christ, they need to grow as disciples of Christ. You will help them in developing their personal relationship with Jesus through prayer and the Word of God. You will guide them to surrender to the authority of Christ so that he becomes their Lord. You will help them begin to develop the character of Christ as they die to self and allow him to live through them.

Chapter Sixteen

$\mathcal{I}$NTRODUCING $\mathcal{P}$EOPLE TO $\mathcal{J}$ESUS $\mathcal{C}$HRIST

One day I walked into the bookstore at the seminary. One of my students grabbed me and said: "Dr. Thompson, I have to conduct a funeral for a lost person, and I desperately need some help. I have never done this before; I am really troubled about it."

I said, "Well, I understand. I will be in my office in about thirty minutes. Come on up, and we will work on it together."

So he came to my office, and we sat down. I said, "I know it is difficult. I have had to conduct funerals for lost people too many times. Who is it?"

"My uncle," he replied.

I said, "Now, let's see, how much time do we have? When is the funeral?"

"I do not know," he replied.

I thought, *Well, the arrangements have not been made yet*, so I said, "Will it be in a couple of days?"

"Oh, no, not necessarily," he answered.

I thought, *Boy, they are going to mummify this guy before they bury him.* I did not tell him that. It would not have been an appropriate thing to say.

So trying very hard to keep my composure, I asked, "What do you mean?"

"He is not dead yet, Dr. Thompson," the fellow replied.

"But you told me it was a funeral for a lost person!"

"Well, he is, but I do not believe he is going to be saved," he said. "People have been praying for him for years. He is an intellectual and just not reachable. Now he has developed emphysema, and his lungs are collapsing."

"I'll tell you what," I said. "I have a better idea. Let's claim Matthew 18:19 for your uncle. Our Lord said, 'If two of you agree on earth about

179

anything that they may ask, it shall be done for them by my Father who is in heaven.'"

"Let's stand between this man and hell and ask God to save him. His problem is not knowledge. His problem is conviction. He needs to realize that he is lost. You cannot convict him. That is the Holy Spirit's job. So let's ask God to engineer circumstances to bring your uncle to Christ."

After we had prayed, I asked, "Has anyone ever confronted him?"

"Well, yes. People have asked him to come to church."

"No," I said, "that is not what I am talking about. Has anyone ever sat down and said, 'Dear friend, I want to tell you the best news that I have ever heard,' and just shared with him who Jesus is and what Jesus did and what it should mean to him. Has he ever been confronted with those three things: his present need, Christ's provision, and an appeal for him to accept what has been done for him?"

"Well," he said. "I do not know if he would listen to me."

I said, "Dear friend, isn't that his decision? What does he have to gain if he does, and what does he have to lose if he does not? He needs to be able to make the choice."

Several weeks later, I saw that student in the hall. He said, "Dr. Thompson, my uncle has been saved. It was the first time I had ever shared the gospel, and he was saved. When I confronted him with the simple truth, do you know what he said?"

I said, "No."

"My uncle said, 'You know I never could buy all of this religion bit because people would never tell me what they were talking about, and I was too proud to ask.'"

That's it. Just talk to people in a normal voice and tell them what Jesus has done for you and can do for them. Confront them with who Jesus is, what sin is, and how God has provided for forgiveness of sin.

As a great, old, Methodist preacher once said, "I heard the gospel, and I heard the gospel, and I heard the gospel, and then one day, praise God, I heard the gospel."

CARING ENOUGH TO CONFRONT

A person has to be convicted by the Holy Spirit; he has to realize that he is lost before he can be saved. He has to see himself as he is in God's sight. When a person stands morally naked before God, he sees himself as God sees him. This is what the Holy Spirit of God does through the

Scriptures and in answer to intercessory prayer. This is the beginning of confrontation.

A time should come when we confront people in our concentric circles. We need to say, "Has there ever come a time in your life when you have come to know Jesus Christ in a personal way, or would you say you are still in the process?" Sometimes we pray and pray. But when God nudges us, when he says it is time to confront them, we need to speak up.

We must confront people with the gospel. You say, "Well, I will just live my life before someone, but I am not good at talking." But you can talk about everything else. You talk about how to bake a cake or tell someone about football. That's no problem!

Two considerations are involved in confronting people with the gospel by just living your life before them. Number one, you are going to have to live a better life than Jesus did because he not only lived the gospel, he talked about it also. Two, if you live a good life and no one knows the source of the power in your life, you have lost the battle.

Sharing the gospel or sharing what Jesus has done in your life should not be a problem. You say, "But I am afraid." I know you are, but do not be afraid. When you begin to pray for people and to love them and meet their needs, the Lord will prepare their hearts. He will prepare yours also. Just simply talk to people about what the Lord means in your life. Share John 3:16, use a gospel tract, use a marked New Testament, or whatever. Then when God does his mighty work in their hearts, they are ready. Do not browbeat people. Just talk to them naturally and in love.

Suppose you are afraid. Let's think about the worst thing that could happen to you. This story may help you to decide.

A CRUSADE IN RENO

Years ago I took five of my laymen to a crusade in California. We were assigned to Reno, Nevada, which is a part of the California Convention. We had a marvelous time. The men who came for us at the air terminal began to prepare us for the crusade immediately.

"Now, brethren, you are not in the Bible Belt," they warned us. "It is hard to witness out here." By the time we reached the general meeting, they had told us five times how difficult it was to witness in Reno. This really built up our confidence!

My five laymen were successful businessmen and knew about the ways of the world. But they were also men who had a great love for God and loved to share him with other people.

181

When we arrived at the meeting, each of us was asked to say a word. But before we did, we were reminded again about how hard it was to witness in Reno. We knew these people needed encouragement.

One of my laymen stood up and said lovingly, "Brethren, we have heard that it is difficult to witness here. I understand that. I am thankful for the work that is going on here. But I want to ask you something. What is the worst possible thing they could do to you?"

There was silence. Then one little boy on the front row stood up and yelled, "Kill ya!"

"How many witnesses have you lost lately?" my layman asked. Everyone laughed and relaxed.

Those five fellows taught me many things that week. They said, "If we have good news to tell, we are going to tell it to anybody who will listen to us." God works when we make ourselves available.

JUST BEING AVAILABLE

One afternoon three of the men were with me driving to the laundromat to do our laundry. All of a sudden, one of the fellows said, "Stop!"

"Why?" I asked, slamming on the brakes.

"There is a lady watering her yard," one answered. "Let's talk to her."

Like paratroopers, all three piled out of the car and encountered this woman in her yard. I stayed in the car. They talked for a while. Then she turned off the water, and they all started toward the house. They motioned for me to come.

I thought to myself, *You're nuts, I have taught you better than to go into a house with a woman by yourselves.* Two teenagers appeared at the door. I was delighted that someone else was home.

I thought, *Oh, boy. Here goes nothing.* I got out of the car, went into the house, and introduced myself. Then I sat down and waited to see what would happen next.

The lady said, "I am so glad you have come. My husband and I separated last week, and it has been torment. My two teenagers have been so upset. We do not belong to a church, and we really have had no one to talk to."

So the fellows shared the gospel. It was a very simple presentation, but it met needs.

The woman said, "Oh, I never understood all of that before. You know, I have been so depressed. I was just out there watering my roses, asking God, if there was a God, 'Can you help me?' Then you walked up."

182

The mother and two teenagers accepted Christ right there. She said they would be at the services that evening.

God was engineering circumstances. God was preparing hearts. But someone had to be available, and someone had to confront.

ONE-ARMED BANDITS IN A GROCERY STORE

At this same time, two other laymen had gone to the store for groceries. One of those fellows could sell ice to the Eskimos.

As the two entered the grocery store, they noticed a fellow sticking money into a "one-armed bandit." In Reno, slot machines are in every grocery store.

One layman walked over to the fellow at the slot machine and said, "That won't pay off!" (Please keep in mind that these men did not get all of their witnessing techniques from me.)

The layman continued, "Seriously, you are wasting your money. I have something that will really pay off!"

"What?" the fellow asked.

My layman said, "Well, let's talk." So all three went outside the store and stood by the car. The layman led the man to the Lord.

As we ate before the service, we all rejoiced over the people who had come to know the Lord that afternoon.

MEETING AT THE ALTAR

About two hundred people attended the evening service. It was glorious. When I gave the invitation, the man from the grocery store came down one aisle and the mother and two teenagers came down the other. They saw each other at the altar. The man from the grocery store was the husband who had separated from the lady and her teenagers. The couple that was separated was reunited in the Lord.

Talk about the Holy Spirit's engineering circumstances! Humanly, how could this problem have been solved? God is in the business of answering prayer. He specializes in it. We make ourselves available by praying: "Father, here I am. Make me a channel to meet the needs of those around me."

LOST WITHOUT CHRIST

Our love for God must precede our love for the lost. If we really love him, we will love the ones whom he loves. We must realize man's lost condition without God. If we believe the Word, then we do not have any option. When the Scriptures say a person is lost without the Lord, that is exactly what they mean. You can bring all the theological speculation to bear that you want. The fact remains: a person without Christ is lost and headed for a Christless eternity in hell.

We often try to water down the gospel, to make it unrejectable. But the thread runs all the way through the Bible: "No one comes to the Father, but through Me" (John 14:6). "There is no other name under heaven that has been given among men, by which we must be saved" (Acts 4:12). "He who has the Son has the life; he who does not have the Son of God does not have the life" (1 John 5:12).

If it did not take the death of Jesus Christ to redeem man, then the cross was a travesty. It was useless. No! He had to come and die. There was no other way. If he is the only way, then men are lost without him. We need to weep over that. A person cannot be changed until he realizes, "Without Christ, I am hopelessly and helplessly lost."

When you begin to think about a mom or dad or child or loved one in Circle 2 or Circle 3, when you think of close friends in Circle 4, or neighbors or associates in Circle 5, acquaintances in Circle 6, and Person X in Circle 7, remember: if they are without Christ, they are lost and condemned to hell. You need to be concerned about their lostness. We do not know how long any of us have. You need to see the urgency of confronting others with the gospel of Jesus Christ.

Jesus said, "What will a man be profited, if he gains the whole world, and forfeits his soul?" (Matt. 16:26). The soul means the totality of the person.

SEEING PEOPLE AS GOD SEES THEM

The closer you get to God, the more you value human life. I will never forget the first day the nurses brought our baby girl to the window for me to see. I looked down and she looked up, and I knew she was thinking, *That's my daddy*. Human life. How precious it is.

One of my colleagues said, "You know, Oscar, I was sitting in the airport in Los Angeles the other day. You can see just about anything and everything in an airport. I was watching people walk and noticing their different clothes, their different smells, and their different looks, and I found myself judging them. Why are they like that? All of a sudden, it dawned on me. I got that nudge from the Lord, 'Careful, my child, I made them.' All of a sudden, I began to see people as God sees them: precious, infinitely precious."

When you talk to someone in one of your inner circles, or your outer circles, perhaps your Circle 7—the person in the grocery store, at the service station, in the jail, or at a restaurant—remember, God made him. He loves him. He wants you to be sensitive to his needs, to care about him.

REJECTING "CHURCHIANITY"

Remember, many people do not reject Christ; they reject a caricature of him. They never really hear the message. How many of you at one time or another rejected a caricature of the Lord? You were rejecting a concept of "churchianity" as you saw it. You were never really confronted with the claims of the person of Jesus Christ and what you needed to do to have fellowship with him.

When you look at any lost person, remember that person has the ability to have fellowship with the God of this universe. We need to think about that.

WHO IS YOUR GOD?

Have we forgotten who our God is? "Father, help me if you can!" we sometimes say. The "if you can" indicates that we've forgotten the all-powerful nature of our God. The very immensity and power of this Sovereign Being is hard for us to comprehend.

The psalmist spent much time talking about the stars, the moon, the sun, and the many other handiworks of God because he realized who God is and what he created.

Light travels at the speed of about 186,000 miles per second. One little boy said, "Man, that will outrun a Chevrolet." Multiply that by sixty and you have one light hour. Multiple that by twenty-four and you have one light day, and then multiply that by three hundred and sixty-five and you have one light year. Light travels about six trillion miles in one light year.

Our nearest star is Alpha Centauri. We cannot see it because it is in the southern hemisphere. However, if you could see Alpha Centauri tonight, you might say, "Look at Alpha Centauri." Actually you would be seeing the light that left Alpha Centauri four and one-third light years ago. That is our nearest star.

Until early in the twentieth century, astronomers thought that the Milky Way was the only galaxy in the universe. It has a diameter of about one hundred thousand light years. They tell us now that there are billions of galaxies. And the one who put everything together, we call Father! But we can only call him Father through Jesus Christ.

Just think, a little finite being created in the image of the God of this universe has the ability to have fellowship with that God every day. For us to neglect to tell people how they can know God is unthinkable.

One night years ago, as I was preaching about these wonders of God that the psalmist talked about, I said, "When God rolls back eternity, Buster, where are you going to be when the 'big show' starts?" Of course, I had no particular person in mind. But during the invitation, a twenty-year-old fellow, tears streaming down his cheeks, came forward. He said, "I'm Buster, and I need to trust Jesus." That is what you call "calling them out."

Do you know the reason the cults and sects are pulling our young people into their groups? It is because the cults find a lonely, troubled, perhaps disillusioned, empty youngster who is not being reached and loved. They say, "We will take care of you. We will love you." The young person is drawn in. We must confront such young people in our concentric circles. We must become the channels of God's love so that these lost people will be drawn to him and his salvation. We must confront in order to make disciples.

PERSONALIZING CHAPTER 16

Using a journal or notebook, respond to the following questions or activities. Record details that will help you understand and apply the truths of this chapter to your own life.

1. Take some time to think about the greatness of the God you love and serve, the One you call heavenly Father. Think about the ways you have experienced his love, his presence, and his power. Then think about how your life would be different if you had never come to know God through Jesus Christ. What would be missing in your life had you never come to know Christ? Pause to praise God and thank him for all he has done in you and for you.

2. Now think about what life must be like for all those in your concentric circles who do not know Christ. How do they face a family crisis? How do they deal with an overwhelming physical or financial need? How do they deal with loneliness, a sense of inferiority, guilt, bitterness, and so forth? What difference could Christ make in their lives? Pause and ask God to help you see the spiritual neediness of those in your concentric circles who do not know Christ.

3. Prepare yourself to share the basic message of the gospel with others when you have the opportunity. Use one or more of the following methods or another you may be familiar with to tell others about the faith you have in Jesus Christ:

- *Personal Testimony:* Prepare to tell others about your life without Christ, how you came to recognize your need for him, how you became a Christian, and what God has done in your life since you turned to him as Savior and Lord.

- *Gospel Tract:* Secure copies of a gospel tract that describes the plan of salvation. Study it so you can read and explain it to a person in your concentric circles who needs to know Christ. Be prepared to give away a copy of the tract when you have finished explaining it to a person.

- *Marked New Testament:* Secure inexpensive copies of the New Testament that have a plan of salvation and Scriptures marked for a person to read and study. Familiarize yourself with how to use the New Testament in sharing the gospel. Be prepared to give away a copy of the New Testament after you have presented the plan of salvation to a person.

- *Video or Movie:* The Jesus film, other movies, and videotapes have the gospel message presented in a very effective way. When you are prepared to share the gospel with people, you can invite them to your home for refreshments and a movie, give (or loan) the video to them for private viewing, and then follow up with a visit, or offer to bring the video by their home so you can watch it together.

- *Memorized Plan of Salvation:* A number of programs are available, which can teach you ways to share your faith effectively. They often help you memorize Scriptures and explanations that will help others understand the claims of Christ on their lives. Study one of these plans so that you can naturally tell another person about God's plan for salvation using Scriptures.

- *A Divine Network:* Everyone can talk about their own experience with Christ in a way that God can use to draw people to himself. However, God has placed you in a body of Christ—your church. Each member is gifted differently so that the whole body can function in a healthy way to make disciples of all peoples. Look to see how God may network you with another person to help others come to Christ. One person may be more gifted at building bridges and showing love, and the other person may be more gifted at telling about the gospel. Remember how John the Baptist pointed Andrew to Christ, and then Andrew brought his brother Peter to Christ. Do you remember the story of the spiritual SWAT team? Find a person or people in your church who can work together with you in sharing the gospel through relationships.

BUILDING UP THE BODY

Use the following questions and activities with your small group to help one another apply these truths to your lives and to build up the body of Christ.

1. Take turns sharing with one another the ways you are prepared to share the gospel with others. Describe ways you have already presented the gospel to other people and how they responded.
2. Identify resources available from your church that can be used to share the gospel with others. You may want to invite your pastor to help equip your group with a variety of ways to witness about your faith.
3. After praying, bridge building, and showing love, what two or three people would you identify as your "Most Wanted"—those for whom you carry the greatest burden, or those who seem to be the closest to coming to Christ? What do you sense God wants you to do next in helping these people come to Christ? How can we pray for you as you seek to obey God in making disciples?
4. What have you done or experienced in the past week as a result of our study thus far? How is God working in your relationships?
5. Ask each small-group member: *How can we pray for you this week?* Then take time to pray for these specific needs or requests.

Chapter Seventeen

ℳaking 𝒟isciples

One semester, as I was listing the marks of a disciple, I said to my class, "Are you teaching your children who have made professions of faith to be disciples?"

Several weeks later, one of my students came to me and said, "During class that day, I thought of my teenagers and how they are in church every service, but as I began to look for that sweet, personal, daily relationship with the Lord, I could not find it in their lives.

"I began to look for other marks of a disciple," Jim continued, "and I realized that I was not building disciples. I was building 'churchgoers.'"

Jim immediately began to intercede for his teenagers. He prayed, "Father, help me to be the kind of father that will help my children become disciples of Jesus Christ. Let them see the characteristics of a disciple in me."

Jim continued, "Several weeks passed. One Sunday night after the service, my fourteen-year-old daughter came to me, put her arms around me, and said, 'Daddy, I want you to know that Jesus has not been real in my life. I want a personal relationship with him like you have. Can you help me?' Now all of that stress and strain between parent and child has dissolved."

COMMISSIONED TO MAKE DISCIPLES

Some day all Christians will give an account of their lives to the Lord. He has given us many commandments by which we are to live. His last commandment, often called the Great Commission, is found in Matthew 28:19–20: "Go therefore and make disciples of all the nations, baptizing them in the name of the Father and the Son and the Holy Spirit, teaching them to observe all that I commanded you; and lo, I am with you always, even to the end of the age."

In these verses, the word that seems to carry the most emphasis is the word *go*. However, this is not true in the Greek. The only Greek imperative in this passage is the word *mateteusate*. The word is derived from the Greek root word *mathetes*, which means "disciple." The other three words, *going, baptizing, teaching,* all participles, derive their force from the imperative, "make disciples." So these two verses in Greek may be translated, "Therefore, as you are going, disciple all nations, baptizing them in the name of the Father and the Son and the Holy Spirit, teaching them to observe all things whatsoever I gave command to you; and behold I am with you all the days until the completion of the age."

We are good at teaching, and we are good at baptizing. But somehow we have lost our central theme. We are not very good at making disciples as we are going.

First, let's clarify several things about these verses of Scripture called the Great Commission. Jesus assumed that we were going. He used a participle, "as you are going," so it is understood that we are going. However, I am afraid that often we have had a reversal of the Great Commission. So often we, as the followers of Jesus, say, "Come and hear" rather than, "As you are going, tell."

Every time I ask my students what the word *disciple* means, I get five dozen different answers. What does *disciple* mean? It will be very difficult to go out and make disciples if we do not have a clear concept of what a disciple is.

WHAT IS A DISCIPLE?

One of the most important terms for a learner in the New Testament comes from *manthanein,* which means "to learn." The word for disciple (*mathetes*) is derived from *manthanein,* meaning that a disciple is a learner.

My daughter Damaris goes to school to "manthano" (I learn or I am taught). It is a teaching relationship between Damaris and her teachers. Next year Damaris will not have the same teachers. The students come and sit in class and learn; then they move on to other teachers.

Most of the teaching in the Jewish world was done in the home and in the scribal schools. In the Greek world, however, it was often done by what we would call peripatetic teachers (*peri* means "around"; *pateo* means "to walk"). The teachers walked from place to place, teaching their particular philosophy. In each place, they gathered a class, taught, extracted a fee for their time, and went on their way. The relationship between teacher and student was much as it is in our day and time. It was simply a relationship of learning.

As already indicated, the word used in the Great Commission is from the Greek word *mathetes,* "disciple." The word *mathetes* embodies several characteristics of a genuine disciple of Jesus Christ. In this chapter we will discuss four of them:

1. A disciple has a personal relationship with the teacher.
2. A disciple is under the total authority of the teacher.
3. A disciple possesses and demonstrates the character of the teacher.
4. A disciple must be prepared to suffer for the teacher.

A DISCIPLE HAS A PERSONAL RELATIONSHIP WITH THE TEACHER

You cannot become a disciple through a correspondence course. A disciple has a personal relationship with the teacher. Can you have a personal relationship with Buddha? Muhammad? Moon? No! Only a handful could. The reason that Jesus went away and the Holy Spirit came was so that he could actually reside in you.

You should not have to go back to a time twenty years ago when you were saved, or look in a baptismal record to see if you have been born again. That is poor discipleship. There needs to be a time when today— not yesterday, not last week—you have fellowship with the living God. That personal and intimate relationship with him is the best indicator that you are a disciple.

I am reminded of the story of a testimony meeting years ago. One woman stood up and sarcastically said, "Well, God saved me forty years ago. My cup has neither gone dry nor has it run over." Then she sat down.

One little boy nudged another little boy on the front row and said, "Yeah, and I bet her cup has wiggle tails in it too." Do not let that happen to you.

Let me remind you of another thing. Just because a person joins your church, is baptized, is on the roll, and attends church does not mean that he has a personal relationship with Jesus Christ. When you are discipling, one of the first things you will want to discover is what that person's relationship is to Jesus. A person will never grow in the Lord until he has a personal relationship with Jesus Christ.

As you are going, you should be careful never to disciple people to yourself. Instead, disciple them to the Lord Jesus Christ. If you disciple people to yourself, they will try to imitate you. They may become very frustrated because they may not have your spiritual gift. They, however, are to bear the character of Jesus Christ through their personality, not yours.

I am not Billy Graham. I do not plan to be. When I was a young preacher, I wanted to be a young Billy Graham. But my pastor said, "Oscar, you are not Billy Graham." I was so disappointed. But I came to realize that God created me to be Oscar Thompson.

While teaching at the seminary, I have been interim pastor at many churches. I was called to a church whose pastor had just resigned. I consider this man to be one of the finest biblical expositors in the world today. We are very close friends. But I was going to follow him. Well, I know who I am, and I know who he is. Someone said, "Isn't it going to be difficult to fill the other pastor's shoes?"

I replied, "I do not intend to try. They will not fit. I am Oscar Thompson. The people will have to accept me as I am, and I am comfortable with the gifts that God has given me. He is sufficient in me."

I am me. I accept me the way I am because God made me. If I can bear his character in my personality, I am comfortable with that. I do not have to be jealous of anyone. I only want to know that I am pleasing to God.

Those of you who are pastors do not need to be intimidated when you follow after a great man of God. Do not be threatened by him or jealous of him or his ministry or the love the congregation has for him. If you are, your ministry will be greatly hindered. You will not be able to do what God intended to do through you. It is only natural that when a man of God leaves a church, the people will love him and continue to love him and talk about him. That has nothing to do with you or their love that will grow for you. Just be yourself, and allow the Lord to live in and through your life. The people will grow to love you too.

A DISCIPLE IS UNDER THE TOTAL AUTHORITY OF THE TEACHER

Being under the total authority of the teacher means that a disciple becomes the personal property of the Lord. It means that you allow Jesus to become Lord of your life. You become Christ-centered. Your life becomes a channel through which God moves and loves and reaches out to people and meets their needs.

You will find the scribes and the Pharisees and others questioning the authority of Jesus, but only once do you find the disciples questioning his authority. The disciples asked him questions and often did not understand what he was saying, but they did not question his authority, except once. Do you remember in Matthew 16:21–23, when Jesus was telling his disciples that he was going to die, and Peter said that he was not? Jesus turned to Peter and said, "Get behind Me, Satan!"

A disciple must recognize that God is the sovereign ruler of the universe. Because he created you, he alone knows what is best for you to get the most out of the life for which he created you. A disciple must submit to his rule, so that God can guide that person to experience the fulfillment he intends for him or her.

A Disciple Possesses and Demonstrates the Character of the Teacher

For a disciple to possess and demonstrate the character of the teacher is essentially what we discussed earlier about the real purpose of life. It is the concept of our bearing his fruit, his life, his ministry, and his love in our lives. The fruit will always reproduce the character of the seed—the seed being the Word of God, the very character of Christ. The spiritual fruit listed in Galatians 5:22–23 will be demonstrated in the life of the believer.

Remember the parable of the sower in Matthew 13:18–23. It explains the different yields of these situations: (1) stolen seed, (2) shallow seed, (3) choked seed, and (4) good seed. As we discussed, the results of bearing fruit are found in John 15:

- upward—answered prayer (v. 7);
- inward—joy (vv. 9–11);
- outward—love (vv. 12–13).

Remember, love is meeting needs.

A Disciple Must Be Prepared to Suffer for the Teacher

Daniel 3 gives us a picture of true discipleship in the midst of suffering. Here Shadrach, Meshach, and Abednego are told that if they would turn from their God and worship the king's golden image, they would not be cast into the fiery furnace. Shadrach, Meshach, and Abednego replied: "O Nebuchadnezzar, we do not need to give you an answer concerning this matter. If it be so, our God whom we serve is able to deliver us from the furnace of blazing fire; and He will deliver us out of your hand, O king. But even if He does not, let it be known to you, O king, that we are not going to serve your gods or worship the golden image that you have set up" (Dan. 3:16–18).

We need to come to the place where we are ready to say, "Father, whatever it costs me, wherever it leads me, I am ready. I am yours. I am going to be faithful, even to death." God has not required most of us in this country to be faithful, even if we have to die for our faith. But we must be willing. The time may come when we will have to make that decision. Around the world, Christians have to make that decision daily. Many thousands die each year because they refuse to renounce their Savior and Lord Jesus Christ.

You may never have to physically die for Christ. But you may have to allow your pride or reputation to die for him. You may need to give up your personal dreams and plans for him. As you love others, you may have to make major sacrifices for him. Have you surrendered your will absolutely to the leadership and lordship of Jesus Christ? Are you a disciple?

I do not know what kind of valleys—disappointments, sorrows, persecutions, or pressures—the Lord is going to let you walk through; but a disciple knows that he is in the hands of his Lord, that nothing can come into his life except by God's permission, and that God will always provide the strength for whatever comes. A disciple can walk through any circumstances in the victory of the Lord.

HELP DISCIPLES GROW

Parents, are you building characteristics of disciples into your children? If you are, you will be much blessed. Are you preparing those youngsters running around at your feet to become disciples, or are you just trying to raise some kids?

If all you have done is raised, educated, and kept your children out of trouble, something is missing in their lives. You are to disciple them. Some of your children may be far from God, and that hurts you. But never lose the hope that someday they will become disciples. Pray for it. Also, remember that they need to see that Jesus is real in your life.

Sunday school teacher, look closer at those people—big or little—in your class. What is your obligation when you teach them on Sunday morning? You are to be making disciples.

Outside the home, the greatest discipling organization in the world is the church. Pastors and staff members, are you making disciples by helping your people grow and mature in Christ? Are you teaching the members of your church to disciple others?

A church might be called "the bunch." I realize that is not couched in the most eloquent of words, but "the bunch" gathers on Sunday morning. What do you do with "the bunch"? Do you browbeat or fuss at them? No! You feed them. You love them. You meet their needs.

As you feed them the Word of God, you will find some people surfacing that hunger to become disciples. I tell my students that if they are preaching God's Word, the cream will rise to the top. Skim the cream and disciple it. If people are being fed the Word, some will desire to become disciples. If the seed is sown, some of it will germinate.

In our concentric circles, everyone has a Jerusalem, a Judea, a Samaria, and a world. Jesus said to start where you are and move forward. Where are you now? Where are you going? Jesus told us to make disciples. Are you?

HELP NEW CHRISTIANS GROW AS DISCIPLES

New Christians need help in establishing a growing love relationship with the Lord. You need to help them become mature believers. Don't think you must do it all by yourself. God has put the church together as a body in a way that all the members have a function in helping the body grow. You and your church can help new believers grow in the following ways:

- Help new Christians get established in a local church and guide them in following the Lord in believer's baptism.
- Teach them to pray. Introduce them to an intimate and personal prayer relationship with their heavenly Father. Help them learn to use different types of prayer like confession, praise, thanksgiving, personal petition, and intercession. Teach them to use the Scriptures in prayer. Encourage them to pray together with other Christians. Help them learn the value of asking others to pray for them.
- Teach them to read and study God's Word on a regular basis. Help them find their way around the Scriptures. Give them a general overview of the Bible.
- Teach them how and why to memorize Scripture. You might begin helping them memorize Scripture that relates to their salvation experience so they can use those same Scriptures in helping others come to know Christ.
- Teach them the importance of obedience to the things God says to them in his Word. Teach them how to gain victory over temptation and how to daily die to sin.
- Teach them how to be reconciled to others, to seek and give forgiveness.
- Teach them how to use the concentric circles pattern to make disciples of their family, friends, neighbors, and associates.

• Teach them to build relationship bridges and show love by meeting needs.

As you point people to Jesus Christ, some are going to turn to him as Lord and Savior. As you help them grow and mature, you are making disciples. You are "teaching them to obey everything" as Christ has commanded you. As you work with new believers, begin right away to help them make disciples too. Probably at no other time in their Christian life will new believers have more lost people in their concentric circles than they do when they become believers. Most often, new believers have a greater zeal and joy because of the love and forgiveness they have just encountered from God. Now is the very best time to help them begin making disciples.

The final stage in making disciples is to help the new believers begin the same process you've been through. The very process of telling others about Christ will cause the new believer to want to know more, obey more, and love more than ever. You can be their encourager and cheerleader as they join God's work of making disciples in their own Jerusalem, Judea, Samaria, and world.

PERSONALIZING CHAPTER [17]

Using a journal or notebook, respond to the following questions or activities. Record details that will help you understand and apply the truths of this chapter to your own life.

1. Take some time to remember the people who helped you grow and mature as a disciple of Jesus Christ. What did they do that was most helpful? What can you learn from their mistakes? Take some time to thank God for those people who discipled you.

2. Ask God how he would grade you as a disciple of Jesus Christ in the following areas and how he would like for you to grow deeper and closer to him in these areas.
   • A disciple has a personal relationship with the teacher.
   • A disciple is under the total authority of the teacher.
   • A disciple possesses and demonstrates the character of the teacher.
   • A disciple must be prepared to suffer for the teacher.

3. Using the list above under "Helping New Christians Grow as Disciples," make your own list of things a new believer would need help in learning and doing to be a mature disciple. What things

were you taught that helped you grow and mature most? What tips or counsel did you receive that was most helpful or meaningful?

4. Make a list of the ways that people helped you grow the most. Were there books you studied that helped? Did you take some classes at church? Did you get "on-the-job training" by participating in certain programs or activities? What did you do that was most meaningful or helpful?

5. Review your concentric circles survey forms. What do you need to be doing to help believers grow and mature (in your family or with others)? Spend time praying for those who are closest to you and who most need to grow and mature in Christ. Ask the Lord to help you know what you should do to join him in making disciples "as you are going." Write notes to yourself regarding the things you sense he is revealing to you.

BUILDING UP THE BODY

Use the following questions and activities with your small group to help one another apply these truths to your lives and to build up the body of Christ.

1. Discuss the ways your church is a "come-and-listen" kind of church or is more an "as-you-are-going-tell" kind of church. What do you sense God wants you to do to be more like the "as-you-are-going-tell" kind of church?

2. What resources and activities does your church provide or make available to help you disciple new believers? What are some ways your church can help members grow into greater depth and maturity as followers of Jesus Christ?

3. What are some of the things you listed while personalizing this chapter that were most meaningful or helpful in the following areas:
   • things that you learned, tips or counsel you received
   • ways, resources, or activities that helped you grow and mature

4. Take some time as a group to evaluate your study:
   • What have you done or experienced during this study of concentric circles that has been most meaningful or helpful?
   • What would you have done differently in the small group time that would have made this a more meaningful or helpful study?
   • Who in your church might benefit from participating in the next session of concentric circles?

- What has God done in your life or the lives of others that has had the greatest impact for Christ's kingdom?

5. As you conclude your study of concentric circles, take time to thank God for what he has taught you and what he has done in and through your lives. Then ask each small-group member: *How can we pray for you in the coming weeks?* Take the time to pray for these specific needs or requests.

Stage 7

Begin Again: Help New Christians Make Disciples

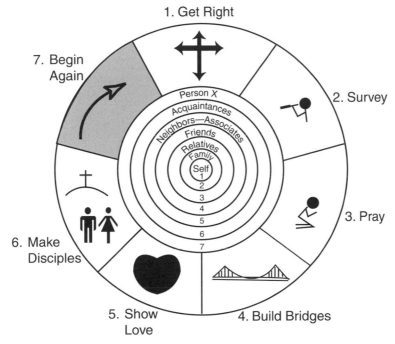

STAGE 7 SUMMARY

HELP NEW CHRISTIANS MAKE DISCIPLES

Making disciples does not end with a decision to follow Christ. That is the beginning. Helping a new Christian grow into a fully devoted follower of Jesus Christ is also a part of the church's assignment in making disciples. The cycle of making disciples doesn't end when a person becomes a Christian. For that person, the cycle begins.

You will be able to help others get right with God, self, and others. You will help them survey, pray, and build bridges to the people in their concentric circles of concern. You can encourage them as they become a channel of God's love. Then you will be able to rejoice with them when they see their loved ones, friends, and associates become disciples of Jesus Christ.

Turn to chapter 1 and begin again with a new believer!

Epilogue

THINGS I HAVE LEARNED

[Oscar Thompson died of cancer in 1980. Prior to his death, God used Oscar to minister to many who were facing terminal illnesses of their own. This epilogue is from a letter that Oscar wrote to cancer patients. Perhaps his insights will be used of the Lord to meet your needs as they have helped many others through the years.]

God's purpose in creating people was to have a vehicle in which to reproduce his life and character. Since Adam, this plan has been thwarted by rebellion and sin. But the miracle of God's redemptive love restores people to a relationship through which God's purpose may be accomplished. He uses every circumstance of life to fashion his children into vessels through which he can pour his love and grace. The following is but a brief glimpse of his working in my life.

In 1976, while on the way to the Southern Baptist Convention in Virginia Beach, Carolyn, Damaris, and I stopped in Washington, D.C. for some sightseeing. That evening I experienced excruciating pain in my right hip. I was taken to the hospital, sedated, and later flown home and hospitalized with a preliminary diagnosis of a slipped disc.

Weeks passed while I lingered in traction, alas, to no avail. In desperation, a spinal fusion was performed. Another two months passed with no relief. Two months later exploratory surgery was performed on the hip.

After surgery I was advised that an inoperable malignant tumor had grown out of the bone. A bone scan later revealed that the malignancy had metastasized and spread to my foot, knee, hip, rib, shoulder, and cranium.

After the doctor left my room that night, a deep, sweet peace from him who is our peace surged within me. It was simply inexplicable and ineffable. I reached for my New Testament on the nightstand and said, "Father, if I am not going to live, I want to count. I need a word from you." There surfaced in my mind a passage of Scripture that I had memorized years before. "Blessed be the God and Father of our Lord Jesus

Christ, the Father of mercies and God of all comfort; who comforts us in all our affliction so that we may be able to comfort those who are in any affliction with the comfort with which we ourselves are comforted by God" (2 Cor. 1:3–4).

"Oh, Father, I understand. You are going to send me through the valley so that I can comfort others with your comfort when they walk there."

Then came that inner nudge that said, "Read on." Verses 8 through 11 revealed this promise to my heart: "We were burdened excessively, beyond our strength, so that we despaired even of life; indeed, we had the sentence of death within ourselves in order that we should not trust in ourselves, but in God who raises the dead; who delivered us from so great a peril of death, and will deliver us, . . . you also joining in helping us through your prayers, that thanks may be given by many persons on our behalf for the favor bestowed upon us through the prayers of many."

I put down the Testament, rejoiced in the Lord, and later slipped into a peaceful, refreshing sleep. Was I rejoicing because I felt I would live? No! I was rejoicing because it really did not matter. My life was under his control. I rejoiced because of a wonderful awareness of his love. Verse after verse that I had memorized began to surface. First John 4:18 exploded in my consciousness: "There is no fear in love; but perfect love casts out fear, because fear involves punishment, and the one who fears is not perfected in love."

I knew that nothing could come into my life without God's permission. If it came with his permission, then I knew that it surely came with his grace to deal with it. Living and dying is not the issue of existence, but rather it is whether he is permitted to reveal his character and life in me.

The joy of living is permitting God to do through us whatever he has in mind for each day. Most people's lives are crucified between two thieves, yesterday and tomorrow. God can only give forgiving grace for yesterday. He stores no provision of grace for tomorrow. Tragically, most of us live in yesterday and tomorrow, in that devastating land of "What if?" God has adequate grace to deal with yesterday if it is put in his hands. But his grace is poured out one day at a time. The person who has not learned this will never live victoriously. He will always be vulnerable to circumstances.

In other words, I learned that God does not give dying grace on non-dying days. To worry about tomorrow is futile as well as sinful. It occupies my time and mind with things God did not intend, thwarting his grace and power in my life.

Today God is permitting me to teach a thousand young seminarians how to share their faith. He is also permitting me to be the channel through which he is comforting those who walk the painful valley of cancer.

My doctors tell me that I am "incredibly normal again." I am not rejoicing that I am well again so much as I am rejoicing in the glorious fact that Jesus is Lord. I can boldly say with the apostle Paul:

"Yes, and I will rejoice. For I know that this shall turn out for my deliverance through your prayers and the provision of the Spirit of Jesus Christ, according to my earnest expectation and hope, that I shall not be put to shame in anything, but that with all boldness, Christ shall even now, as always, be exalted in my body, whether by life or by death. For to me, to live is Christ, and to die is gain. But if I am to live on in the flesh, this will mean fruitful labor for me; and I do not know which to choose. But I am hard-pressed from both directions, having the desire to depart and be with Christ, for that is very much better; yet to remain on in the flesh is more necessary for your sake. And convinced of this, I know that I shall remain and continue with you all for your progress and joy in the faith, so that your proud confidence in me may abound in Christ Jesus" (Phil. 1:18–26).

PRAISE HIM.

DATE ENTERED:_____

CONCENTRIC CIRCLES
SURVEY FORM*

Circle #

STAGE 2: SURVEY

Name: _____

Address: _____

City, State, Zip _____

Home Phone: _____ Work Phone: _____

Relationship

Status: ❑ Single ❑ Married ❑ Divorced ❑ Widowed ❑ Separated

Family Members (Name & Relationship)

_____

_____

STAGE 3: PRAY

Prayer Partner: _____ Phone: _____

Specific Prayer Request / Needs / Circumstances

_____

_____

_____

_____

_____

STAGE 4: BUILD BRIDGES

Birthday: _____ Anniversary: _____

Occupation/place of employment: _____

Hobbies/interests: _____

Times of Joy or Stress to Remember (and date):

_____

_____

_____

_____

Strategy: _____

SWAT Team helpers: _____

STAGE 5: SHOW LOVE

Needs (physical, emotional, mental, family, financial):

_____

_____

_____

Spiritual Needs: _____

_____

STAGE 6: MAKE DISCIPLES

Confrontation and Seed-Sowing Strategy: _____

_____

Date and Way Gospel Presented: _____

Response: _____

Discipleship Helps or Strategy for New Believer: _____

_____

_____

_____

STAGE 7: BEGIN AGAIN

Plan to Study *Concentric Circles of Concern:* _____

_____

Date started: _____

* You have permission from publisher to reproduce this form for personal use in your Concentric Circles survey.

DATE ENTERED: 4-2-99

CONCENTRIC CIRCLES
SURVEY FORM*

Circle #

③

STAGE 2: SURVEY

Name: Susan Galloway

Address: 1232 Banner Drive

City, State, Zip: Bethel, OK 74724

Home Phone: 405-241-0165   Work Phone: —

Relationship

Status: ☐ Single ☐ Married ☐ Divorced ☒ Widowed ☐ Separated

Family Members (Name & Relationship)

Bill Galloway (son)

husband was Benton

STAGE 3: PRAY

Prayer Partner: Robert Lewis   Phone: 904-2771

Specific Prayer Request / Needs / Circumstances

1. Comfort in loss of husband
2. Give me descernment about her spiritual condition
3. Forgiveness/Reconciliation regarding church split 30 years ago.
4. Opportunity to visit Aunt Susan this summer.

STAGE 4: BUILD BRIDGES

Birthday: 8-14-23   Anniversary: 10-4-48

Occupation/place of employment: Retired

Hobbies/interests: Flower gardening

Times of Joy or Stress to Remember (and date):

Lost husband   12-7-98

Strategy: Write letters, send cards, call

SWAT Team helpers: _____

Stage 5: Show Love

Needs (physical, emotional, mental, family, financial):

Grieving — sent Good Grief   4-2-99

lonely

Spiritual Needs: hasn't been active in church in
30 years

Stage 6: Make Disciples

Confrontation and Seed-Sowing Strategy: _____

_____

Date and Way Gospel Presented: _____

Response: _____

Discipleship Helps or Strategy for New Believer: _____

_____

_____

_____

Stage 7: Begin Again

Plan to Study *Concentric Circles of Concern:* _____

_____

Date started: _____

* You have permission from publisher to reproduce this form for personal use in your Concentric Circles survey.